# Vedic Astrology

Introduction To The Origins And Core Concepts Of Jyotish

*(Ancient Teachings For The Soul Relationships Self-Esteem)*

**Thomas Barnes**

Published By **John Kembrey**

## Thomas Barnes

All Rights Reserved

*Vedic Astrology: Introduction To The Origins And Core Concepts Of Jyotish (Ancient Teachings For The Soul Relationships Self-Esteem)*

# ISBN 978-1-77485-633-8

No part of this guidebook shall be reproduced in any form without permission in writing from the publisher except in the case of brief quotations embodied in critical articles or reviews.

Legal & Disclaimer

The information contained in this ebook is not designed to replace or take the place of any form of medicine or professional medical advice. The information in this ebook has been provided for educational & entertainment purposes only.

The information contained in this book has been compiled from sources deemed reliable, and it is accurate to the best of the Author's knowledge; however, the Author cannot guarantee its accuracy and validity and cannot be held liable for any errors or omissions. Changes are periodically made to this book. You must consult your doctor or get professional medical advice before using any of the suggested remedies, techniques, or information in this book.

Upon using the information contained in this book, you agree to hold harmless the Author from and against any damages, costs, and expenses, including any legal fees potentially resulting from the application of any of the information provided by this guide. This disclaimer applies to any damages or injury caused by the use and application, whether directly or indirectly, of any advice or information presented, whether for breach of contract, tort, negligence, personal injury, criminal intent, or under any other cause of action.

You agree to accept all risks of using the information presented inside this book. You need to consult a professional medical practitioner in order to ensure you are both able and healthy enough to participate in this program.

Table Of Contents

Introduction _____ 1

Chapter 1: What Exactly Is Vedic Astrology?_____ 4

Chapter 2: Sun (Surya) _____ 45

Chapter 3: Twelve Houses And Their Meanings _____ 69

Chapter 4: How To Cast The Birth Chart _____ 89

Chapter 5: Retrograde (Vakra) Planets _____ 108

Chapter 6: Aspects (Drishti) On Planets And Their Impact On The Planets. _____ 125

Chapter 7: Diffrent Yoga In Birth Chart _____ 139

## Introduction

The solar System consists of the Sun and the other planets that revolve around the Sun. There are nine planets which are typically considered for reasons of astronomy. Scientists claim that they are able to have discovered the tenth planet that has yet to be known as. Sun can be described as a star that has its own light source. Other planets receive their illumination directly from the Sun. The planets that make up the Solar System are Mercury, Venus, Earth, Mars, Jupiter, Saturn, Uranus, Neptune and Pluto. Certain planets have natural satellites that revolve around the planet. In our instance, Moon serves as our primary satellite, and it is the closest celestial body to Earth. So, the impact it has on human beings is significant. The word"planet" is derived of its Greek term 'planetes' which literally is a reference to wanderers. However it is believed that the Hindu idea of Planet is called 'Sam Bhavate Sam Grah', which refers to "that that influences the world is known as Grah". The impact of the planets on our lives is being studied by the open-minded scientists community. It is a known fact that cyclones, high tides and floods are usually observed to be occurring on the full moon. It was further established by recent research regarding the subject of Earthquakes. It has been discovered that it typically occur during eclipse. The reason for this is because when the eclipse occurs, the Sun, Moon and the earth are in an identical plane. This means that the gravitational pull is at its highest at that moment in time.

Astrological Understanding:

According to "Brihat Parashara-Hora Shastra" (Chapter 2 verses 3-4) There are numerous incarnations of the Lord who is not born Janardhan (or Vishnu. He has taken on the form of Navgrahas or planets in order to confer on living beings the outcomes that they have wrought through their Karmas or actions. He took on the auspicious shape of Grahas in order to destroy the power of demons, and to maintain the power that is the Devas (the divinity) in order to establish Dharma (religion and faith).

Rama is the embodiment of Sun, Krishna of the Moon, Narasimha of the Mars, Buddha that of Mercury, Vamana that of Jupiter Parashurama is from Venus Koorma is Saturn. Varaha which is comes from Rahu and Meena the incarnation is from Ketu. Other incarnations also come from the planets and stars. The ones who have more Parmatmamsa are referred to as divine beings or divine beings.

If we are talking about Vedic Astrology, we leave out planets such as Uranus, Neptune and Pluto and also include the two Chaya Grah (Shadowy Planets) specifically Rahu as well as Ketu. The reason for this is because you consider that the all-knowing Parashara along with other Rishis did not take them into consideration, it is not a reason to consider the same view. The planets Rahu and Ketu have the same effect. The reason that these planets are not in the picture is because they are within only one Rashi (Sign) over quite a long period. Sometimes, for decades or further, these planets are extremely distant from Earth. Thus, their effects are not something to be taken into consideration. In addition, without the benefit of a classical foundation, it wouldn't be prudent to take them into consideration. Astrology is the study of the sun as well as Moon as planets. All our observations are based on Geo- Central Observations that consider the Earth as the centre to the entire universe.

## Chapter 1: What Exactly Is Vedic Astrology?

Vedic Astrology is a science of light. It is a science of light. Astrology (Jyotish) has its roots founded on the textual texts from India known as the Veda. The origins of the Veda are obscured in the mists of time. Additionally, there is an immense amount of information which is written down and passed down within astrological families, as well as of the Veda. Vedic Astrology is deep rooted in spiritual practices. Jyotish is also known as the eye, or the light of the Veda. It's a method of learning more about yourself and gaining confirmation of the place you've been on your journey to Self realisation. This is because it reveals how you've created patterns that are both beneficial and destructive. It also provides the motivation and confidence to continue to progress in better and more effective ways when utilized correctly. It is not all on our own. There are numerous ways to connect us to our souls and God for example: reflection or meditation, prayer, particularly with people who share similar thoughts as well as yoga practices for meditation, and also giving to and helping other people.

Based on current scientific calculations Jyotish is a side-realistic based. It means that calculations based on astronomy consider the equinox's precession when determining where the celestial constellations from the Zodiac planets are located.

It is a Vedic method of studying Astrology can be described as the investigation of what can help you shine and help you fulfil your destiny on earth, and fulfill the reason for the first place and in being born. In the real world, Vedic astrology also focuses on ways to eliminate or bypass or overcome obstacles that block your bright light from shining.

The aim the purpose of Astrology is to assist us focus our spirit on the way ahead, so that we can see the way of life. Astrology can be used in conjunction in conjunction with Yoga as well as Ayurveda. It is believed that Jyotisha guides us on the right path, Ayurveda keeps us healthy while walking the path, as well. Yoga (in its many variations) is the best way to take the right path. They all function together and share the same philosophical basis. Astrology can assist in finding the appropriate yoga branch to study, and it can aid in the creation of an Ayurvedic regimen that can stop diseases that haven't occurred yet.

Astrology requires a lot of time to master, but it is a pathway that opens the eyes to comprehend the interconnectedness of all things in a synchronized universe.

## 2. TWELVE Zodiac Signs (Rashi) and their significance

### Aries (Mesha)

Aries is an ebullient sign that is ruled by Mars as the symbol of energy. The Sun is elevated by this sign. Saturn is weak under this sign. The head is the brain's primary concern in this sign. In the event that Mars along with Mercury are both strong and strong, the Aries ascendant has good health. Also, they are not afflicted by illnesses that cause inflammation, fevers and headaches. They also suffer from wounds anxiety, insomnia, mental tension diseases of blood that are impure and bilious illnesses, such as short-Tempe-redness constipation, stammering etc. Aries is a sign of mooltrikon, a Mars. Aries are extremely energetic, powerful, and active and healthy when Mars is powerful. For Aries ascendant The Ishta Devata (for worshiping and meditation) is goddess of the gods, mother divine Durga.

Aries is a positive male, rajasic volatile, pitta brutal, barren and quadruped. Based on the influence on ascendant or Mars the sign Aries makes their natives enthusiastic skilled, independent and competent in their activities leading, and becoming leaders with perseverance, determination aggressive, impetuous combatants, courageous strong, confident, courageous mental clarity, competitive and energised as well as strong-willed and visionary. aggressive, offensive, argumentative and irritable. insecure and self-centered. For Aries ascendant and Mars, their influence from Saturn is a force for building and turns them into entrepreneurs. They are able to make lots of money through their own efforts. Based on the strength of Mars as the most important determinant of work as well as the Sun ruling intelligence and being a general significator of career success as well as the Moon controlling education. Arian are commanders in chief, dentists, executives, executioners and gangsters, producers as well as paramilitary and military forces, police forces, project surgeons, erectors, professions that require fire and metals and more. Influence of the other planets in the tenth, first or second house alters the career options.

Taurus (Vrisha)

Taurus is a sign of earth which is ruled by Venus as the symbol of materialism and the pursuit of conveniences. The Moon is elevated within this sign. Ketu is debilitated under this sign. These aspects make Taurus ascendants the appearance of being materialistic sensual, maternal and loving who enjoy comfort, beauty and luxury in their surroundings believing that they are in the right. If Taurus is the ascendant then Taurus's Ishta Devata (for worshiping and meditation) is Lord Vishnu. The sign of the face governs its organs, the neck the cervical region, bones, cerebellum , and facial bones. If Venus as the ruler of the house in the sixth is strong, Taurus ascendants have excellent health. If not, they're weak constitution, suffer from digestive problems, diseases of the eyes, throat teeth, etc. and illnesses that are mostly caused by a the weak vein system. In the event of an excess consumption, it could be the cause of poor health.

Taurus can be described as a fixed negative, rajasic, vata female mild, semi-fruitful, and quadruped astrological sign. It is an exact and temperate character. Based on the influence of the ascendant, Taurus generally makes its natives more cautious, prudent permanent, unchanging, determined in their methods, able and gentle, becoming excellent communicators, planners, and persevering, analytical, simple sophisticated, attractive romantic, patient affectionate, tender, romantic and charming, or forceful and possessive and naive and resentful. emotional, lazy and avid pleasure-seekers. The force of Saturn as the most important determinant of career and the Sun controlling education and being a general significator of professional success and the Moon being the ruler of business, Taurus ascendants become businessmen and engineers, designers technologist and industrialists. They also do administrative work as well as housekeepers. Other planets' influence in the tenth, second or first houses alters the career options.

Gemini (Mithuna)

Gemini is a sign of air which is ruled by Mercury as the significator of confidence and communication. These elements provide Gemini ascendants exceptional abilities in communication and speech. They are a dynamic species and are constantly seeking movement, change, exchange and ingenuity. The native is able to grow in the realm of spirituality if their mind is directed inwards. If Gemini is the sign that ascends and it is believed that the Ishta Devata (for worshiping and meditation) could be the goddess of worship goddess Lakshmi. The Gemini sign governs the ears, necks shoulder and hands, as well as arms nervous and respiratory systems, bronchial tube, collar and shoulder bones, bones of the arms and hands. Because both the ascendant and sixth houses don't have mooltrikona, the Sun as the symbol of vitality, is regarded as the primary factor in the health of Gemini ascendants.

When the Sun is healthy and healthy, they are in healthy health. If not, Gemini ascendants have a weak constitution and suffer from chronic headaches, high blood pressure, and respiratory illnesses as well as asthma, problems with the nervous system and depression that can cause partial paralysis and stammering. They also suffer from shoulder pain, swollen shoulders and more.

Gemini is an astrological dual positive tri-dosha i.e. pitta, vatta and kapha, male active, shy and bipedal sign that reveals an enthusiastic personality with creative concepts. They generally love learning and are a fan of motion and change, as well as initiative. Based on the influences that affect the ascendant, Gemini generally presents its natives with a keen intellect and a lucid mind capable of being spontaneous, flexible analytical, educated skilled, knowledgeable with teaching skills as well as wit, humor and imagination, or anxious, restless, and unsure. The power of Mercury as the planet of education, Moon as the most important determinant of work and the Sun being the ruler of entrepreneurial spirit and a general indicator of the success of a profession, Gemini ascendants become accountants auditors, advisors writers, authors and communicators, businessmen computer programmers, engineers skilled in analysis work, journalists, intellectuals poets, lawyers and publishers, salesmen secretary and computer engineers, government services and so on. Other planets' influence in the tenth, the first or second houses alters the work-related pursuits.

Cancer (Karka)

Cancer is a sign of water typically weak, and controlled by the Moon that is mutable in its nature, and also soft. Jupiter is elevated by this sign. Mars is weakened within this sign. This makes Cancer ascendants loving and nurturing extremely emotional, sensitive gentle and thoughtful. If Cancer is ascending and it is believed that the Ishta Devata (for worshiping and meditation) is Lord Shiva. This sign is associated with the chest, rib cage the heart, lungs, and the breasts. In the event that your Moon as well as Jupiter are healthy, Cancerians have good health. They also suffer from a sluggish constitution and ugly appearance. They are also afflicted with physical illnesses, mental disorders, of chest, breasts and heart, epigastria region circulation and lymphatic congestion, jaundice, and other liver issues, etc. The sign of the Moon is called mooltrikon. the Moon.

Cancer is a moving negative, satvic female, kapha fruitful, multiples and mute sign that symbolizes intelligence and grace. The influence on the ascendant or the Moon this sign Cancer typically makes their people excellent hosts, capable of flexibility and receptivity compassionate, peace-loving with wit, humor and imagination. They can also be overly emotional sensitive, shy, emotionally unstable, dependent and attached. Because the Moon is a volatile planet and is often weak or in pakshabala or by moving to houses of malefic in the ascendant, or being young or older age, or moving to the debilitation sign, either in navamsa or in rashi or by being in the mooltrikona sign on any planet weak, Cancer ascendants can be unchanging in their behaviour. Based on the strength of Mars and the Sun as the main career determinants and the Moon to ensure a steady profession, Cancer ascendants become administrators and public relations managers. They are nurses, healers and housekeepers hoteliers, restaurant proprietors catering professionals, cooks food establishment owners, professional who deal with liquids, etc. Other planets' influence on the tenth first or second house alters the work-related pursuits.

Leo (Singha)

Leo is an ebullient sign that is which is ruled by the Sun which is the symbol of energy, intelligence male progenitors, prestige and social status. These aspects give Leos hearty with character and power. For Leo ascendants, the Ishta Devata (for worshiping and meditation) could be the goddess of the gods, mother divine Durga. This sign governs the stomach, stomach, the upper part of the spinal cord, spine back the gall bladder, liver as well as the pancreas, spleen and spleen. When the Sun is strong, Leos have good health. They also are prone to heart diseases and back, spine bones, spleen liver, pancreas stomach, digestive problems and fevers etc. And they lack energy and strength. This is known as the mooltrikona sign from the Sun.

Leo is an unchanging, positive, male, satvic, pitta gentle, generous, barren, and quadruped sign . It, when it rises in the ascendant with a powerful Sun it makes one appear wealthy, noble and gives a stunning appearance. They are the center of the spotlight. Based on the influences of the ascendant or the Sun, Leo is a sign that Leo provides intelligence, a determination, a strong will as well as a sense of authority and determination, which makes their people adept, patient listeners rulers, aristocratic persistent, dramatic and courageous or dominant, authoritative and awe-inspiring as well as impatient, jealous persistent, demanding, angry and impulsive. Since Mercury is the main determinant of professional life and the Sun is a general indicator of professional success and Venus governs the entrepreneurial side depending on their strengths, Leos may join a high-ranking government position that provides security and a fixed earnings, and may also earn from recreation, sport or other scientific endeavors and may also be the head of large groups as administrators, organizers or leaders, contractors or politicians. They would prefer to work for themselves and won't be averse to subordination. The influence of planets on the tenth the first or second house, alters the career options.

Virgo (Kanya)

Virgo is considered to be an earthly sign that is ruled by Mercury who is the governor of the nervous system. Mercury is elevated in this sign. Venus is weak. These aspects give Virgos an observant nature and a deep sense of sensuality. For mercury ascendants they are it is believed that the Ishta Devata (for worshiping and meditation) could be Lord Vishnu. Virgo is the ruler of the abdomen, waist region, as well as the nervous system, including the small intestine, the upper portion of the large intestine. It also controls the kidneys and appendix. In the event that Mercury as well as Saturn are healthy, Virgos have good health. If they are not, they can develop hypochondriacs and are susceptible to nervous breakdown, over-exertion appendicitis, constipation and so on. It's the mooltrikona symbol of Mercury.

Virgo has a dual negative, tamasic, vata female, barren, and biped sign. And, if Mercury is powerful, it grants the ability to analyze and discrimination. Based on the influences of the ascendant or Mercury, the sign of Virgo typically makes their people friendly attractive, charming, shrewd careful, protective, trustworthy, reliable honest, true practical, sincere, sensitive or critical, neurotic distant, resentful impatient and nitpickers with a tendency to find faults. Because Mercury is in transit through a region of 28 degrees, both sides of the Sun and for a long period of time during the year, it is in a state of combust and weakness. Then it enters the state of debilitation every year for around 1 month. It then goes to old age and infancy about 12 times in a year, besides being under the influences by Rahu, Ketu and other maletic planets with a functional role in the natal chart. The typical weak point of Mercury makes people born in the Virgo sign feel anxious in life. They're generally anxious and require support to maintain confidence in their own abilities. If the chart of natal Mercury can be weak. The person is afflicted with noticeable veins, lacks wit and lacks charm. In accordance with the strengths of Venus and Mercury, Sun as well as Mercury, Virgos become accountants artisans, artists draftsmen, teachers engineers, mathematicians, traders and writers, among others. They are suited to jobs that require meticulous work. The influence of planets other than the tenth on the tenth house, the first or second houses can alter the work environment.

Libra (Tula)

Libra is a soaring sign which is ruled by Venus who is the symbol for materialism and conveniences. Saturn is elevated in this sign, and the Sun is weak. If the Sun that governs the soul is in this sign, which governs pleasures and luxuries, the spiritual growth of the person is blocked and this is the reason why the Sun is weakened within this particular sign. If Saturn is located in this sign, it is elevated because Saturn is the ruler of servants and occupies the sign of luxury and pleasures. These elements make Libras the most attractive persona, when Venus is powerful. In the event that Libra is ascendant in the sky, it is believed that the Ishta Devata (for worshiping and meditation) could be goddess Lakshmi. This sign governs the lumbar region and the lumbar bones, skin lower part of the large intestinal tract, bladder, and the inside sexual organs, such as the uterus, ovaries, testicles and the prostate gland. If Venus is healthy, Libras are healthy and in good shape. They also are not susceptible to ailments that affect the areas of this sign, diabetes, skin conditions venereal kidney problems and urination issues Gout pains, arthritis, and more. This is the Mooltrikona signification of Venus.

Libra is a movable positive, rajasic and tri-dosha male semi-fruitful, friendly and bipedal sign. It is a symbol of clarity, justice, strong willpower, and optimism. It is extremely sensitive. In accordance with the influences of the ascendant or Venus this sign Libra generally gives their people an intense sense of justice, harmony balanced, beauty, and anesthetic sense. This makes them spontaneous, creative charismatic, harmonious and compassionate, as well as self-reliant, flexible optimistic, talkative, thinking and capable of evaluating diverse perspectives and judgement, or unreliable, inconstant, and undecisive. Based on the strengths of the Moon as well as Venus, Sun as well as Venus, Libras become actors as well as actresses, financial advisers hoteliers, legal advisers and musicians, managers, doctors and many more. They enjoy public careers.

Influence of planets in the tenth first or second houses alters the work environment.

Scorpio (Vrishchik)

Scorpio is a sign of water which is ruled by Mars which is the significator of energy. The sign is fragile. Ketu is elevated in this sign, and the Moon is weak. This makes Scorpios more logical and rigid. To be a Scorpio ascendant The Ishta Devata (for worshiping and meditation) could be Lord Shiva. The Scorpio sign governs the the outer reproductive organs and scrotum anus, rectum, the pelvic bones and nasal organs. If Mars as the ruler of the house of sixth is strong, Scorpios are small in stature well-built and in healthy health. They also have an unhealthy constitution and are afflicted with the aforementioned boils, urinary tract infections, and surgeries, all ruled by Scorpio.

Scorpio is a fixed, negative male, kapha, rajasic muted as well as a violent, fruitful, and multiples sign that evokes serious emotions. The influence on the ascendant, Scorpio generally renders the people disciplined, focused confident, self-restrained, frightened and persevering, as well as active, intense, energetic and self-centered. They are decisive as well as tough and straightforward. They can also be extremely sensitive, introverted insecure, and ready to defend themselves.

Based on the strengths that is attributed to and the strength of Sun or Jupiter, Scorpios become administrators advocates, advocates, chemists detectives, officers of their Armed Forces, policemen, surgeons, politicians trading in chemicals and metals, and so on. Influence of the other planets in the tenth, first or second house alters the career options

Sagittarius (Dhanu)

Sagittarius is an ebullient sign that is which is ruled by Jupiter as the god of luck and wisdom. Sagittarius ascendants are driven keen to learn and have an excellent sense of judgement. If Sagittarius is the ascendant and this Ishta Devata (for worshiping and meditation) is Goddess Durga. This sign governs hips and the thighs, as well as the arterial system, nerves and the ear. If Jupiter is strong, Sagittarians are healthy. They also are prone to anemia, digestive problems flatulence, diseases of the liver/gall bladder, jaundice high fevers diabetic rheumatism, diabetes and problems with the hips and thighs. The native could also be afflicted with problems due to his tendency to indulge in excessive drinks and food. It is the sign of mooltrikona of Jupiter.

Sagittarius can be described as a double positive and negative, satvic, pitta male, semi-fruitful, the first half biped and second the quadruped sign, which indicates an impressive personality. The first portion of Sagittarius is human , while the second portion is quadruple. Based on the influence of the ascendant or Jupiter the sign of Sagittarius typically makes its natives people who love nature, goal-oriented charming, generous, joyful and organized. They are quick-witted philosophical, self-righteous or nit-pickers, intolerant, easily annoyed and reckless. People born in this sign can be found in positions of training or as advisors due to their friendly nature and analytical mind. Based on the strengths of Mercury, Jupiter and Saturn ascendants of Sagittarius, they are suited to advisory roles and can become entrepreneurs, trainers for jobs such as financial advisors, lawyers and lawyers, teachers, religious leaders, doctors and many more. Influence of the other planets in the tenth, first or second house alters the profession.

Capricorn (Makara)

Capricorn is a sign of earth which is ruled by Saturn which is the significator of responsibility and duty. Mars is elevated in this sign while Jupiter is weak. These elements make Capricorn ascendants the traits of hardworking, ambitious and self-centered. This is a sign of a practical realization. For Capricorn ascendants The Ishta Devata (for worshiping and meditation) could be Lord Vishnu. This sign governs knees, joints, kneecaps, skin and joints. Since both the ascendant and the sixth house are not ruled by mooltrikona, the Sun is the symbol for vitality, is regarded as the most important factor in the health of Capricorn ascendants. If their Sun is healthy and healthy, they will be in healthy health. In other cases, Capricorn ascendants have a poor constitution and suffer from joint pains, inflammation as well as general weakness, a weak body, skin disorders and allergies,. Capricorn ascendants may also suffer from problems resulting from excessive work and neurological conditions.

Capricorn is a movable negative, tamasic, vata female, semi-fruitful half quadruped and the second half footless sign. It signifies the cheating, tact, lethargy and melancholy in the event that Saturn does not perform well in Nativity. Capricorn rising is attractive when Saturn can be strong. The natural benefics aspect to the ascendant adds an attractive appearance to the person. The negative influence on weak Saturn as Lord of the house second can give the appearance of an individual who has advanced in age, with sunken eyes, wrinkled bodies and more. The first part of Capricorn is a bit watery, while the second portion is earthy. Depends on the influences that affect the ascendant, Capricorn typically blends dedication and perseverance as well as flexibility, adaptability and flexibility. This gives their people a traditional, calm, and cautious and thrifty. They are also traditional methodical, social practical, with organizational capability, faithful cautious, protective reliable and persistent or self-centered rigid and angry. Based on the strengths of Venus as well as or the Sun as well as Saturn, Capricorn ascendants become entrepreneurs, agriculturists, lawyers, political leaders, and others. They are cautious about their finances. The influence of planets on the 10th, the first or second house, alters the professions.

Aquarius (Kumbha)

Aquarius is a soaring sign which is ruled by Saturn which is the symbol of responsibility and duty. These elements make Aquarians self-sufficient and willing to challenge accepted norms of conduct when they believe that doing so are morally right. For Aquarius ascendant The Ishta Devata (for worshipping and meditation) is goddess of the gods, mother divine Lakshmi. This sign is associated with ankles, calves and shanks as well as shin bone blood circulation, and so on. In the event that Saturn as well as the Moon are healthy, Aquarians are healthy and in good shape. They are also prone to infections and colds, and are prone to fractures in the lower leg, as well as cancerous illnesses and injuries as well. within the areas of the world ruled by Aquarius. Arthritis and rheumatism can also be caused by the advancing age. It is the Mooltrikona signification of Saturn.

Aquarius is an unchanging positive, positive, tamasic tri-dosha male, fruitful biped, talkative sign and represents qualities such as the integrity, ideals, compassion and more. According to the power of its god. The description of the body is similar to Saturn i.e. large stature, a slim body, and with prominent veins, if Saturn is robust. The influence on the ascendant or Saturn the sign of Aquarius typically makes its natives willing to help, friendly with initiative, persistent and focused on work attentive, friendly, thoughtful with a plethora of innovative ideas, adamant, compassionate and abrasive and scientific. They are also compassionate, creative and innovative or rigid, impervious and ineffective. The strength of Saturn and its influence on the Sun or Mars, Aquarius ascendants become industrialists as well as leaders of the marginalized or servants, writers, thinkers as well as religious instructors. Influence of the other planets in the first, tenth or second houses alters the work-related pursuits.

Pisces (Meena)

Pisces is a sign of water that is ruled by Jupiter who is the symbol of luck and knowledge. Venus is the symbol of things of the world and luxury is elevated. Mercury as the significator of intelligence, is weakened within this sign. This makes the Pisceans romantic creative, imaginative, compassionate and generous. To be a Pisces ascendant this Ishta Devata (form of god to be worshipped and meditate) is Lord Shiva. This sign governs feet and toes, the lymphatic system toe bones,, and toes. If the Sun as the Lord of the 6th house is strong, the Pisces are healthy. If not, they've got a poor constitution, and suffer from joint pains, gout-related pains and conditions related to the lymphatic system, blood circulation feet, toes, bones of the feet/toes and so on.

It is also a double negative and satvic, female muted, fruitful, and a footless sign, which symbolizes pleasure, sensitivity and sensitivity, among other things. Based on the influence on the ascendant, Pisces generally gives their natives a soft, joyful, compassionate and caring, dedicated to duty, emotionally, enthusiastic optimistic, impressionable, sensitive, morally minded and a philosophical, mystical emotional and compassionate or vulnerable, timid as well as indolent and easy to love. Based on the strengths of Jupiter and Mars, the Sun as well as Mars, Pisces ascendants join the fields of development, commerce, legal advisor, financial advisor, training, and so on. They excel in their field and has a generous nature. The influence of planets in the tenth the first or second house, alters the work-related pursuits.

## 3. NINE Planets and their signification
### Sun (Surya)

The Sun is the most powerful over all the planets. It's the source of light and life to every body. It represents fatherhood who is responsible to bring into existence and supporting the new baby in the world. This is why the Sun symbolizes the father figure and vitality. When the Sun is robust in a birth that means the energy and fatherhood will assist the baby to improve their health in a healthy way. The Sun is also a symbol of the King, the master of the state, the president of the country, and the head of nation and highly-placed people such as administrators, contractors and chairmen of medical institutions, industrial establishments pharmacists, chemists politicians, bureaucrats, police and social status progeny, male children and is a secondary symbol for husbands. The Sun is represented as a doctor and king When it is strong, it signifies top administrative positions in the administration, politics physicians in medicine and so on. confidence, self-confidence dignity, nobility power, splendor, prestige and trust and generosity. It also signifies the power of authority, authority, leadership , and innovation.

The Sun is male-dominated, dry, hot, and constructive as satvic, pitta and has strong bones. The Sun's nature is noble, kind as well as cruel. Its temperament is stable and constant. The Sun is a square-shaped body, magnificent appearance, powerful words, can make a person brave and grants administrative abilities. Its color is blood red and governs pink, orange and gold colors and the element of fire fiery or pungent tastes as well as the perception of sight, Sundays, the direction of east copper, gold, ruby temples, deserts, palaces, government structures, and towers.

The Sun is the symbol of the head, body soul, ego, determination and self-realization. health bone structure, constitution blood, brain digestion fire, bile Organ of the voice and heart as the life-centre. male right eye, as well as left in the the case of females. If it is not strong in an nativity, it causes poor eyesight, headaches and digestive problems, irregular blood circulation, heart problems dental issues bone fractures, fevers as well as high blood pressure, neuralgia, hair loss bone cancer, a insufficient immune system and more. and symbolizes pride, self-centeredness, egotism pride, pomp, ostentation, and the power of despotism. The Sun is a significator planet of vitality and life giving in any nativity because it governs the digestive system, which supplies nourishment for the entire body. Since the soul is healthier and more easily elevated if you are in good health, the Sun also symbolizes the soul. Sun is a significator for health, wealth and prosperity. Sun is also a symbol for inheritance, employment and mental abilities, profession and comforts, as well as intelligence, quick gains, general luck and more advanced education and spiritual learning and the spiritual world.

Moon (Chandra)

It is believed that the Moon is the supreme of the solar system. After the Sun it is the Moon's role to play. the Moon is crucial because it represents motherhood. Motherhood is the primary role of a child, and is the primary teacher of the child. This is the reason why the Moon is a symbol of mind. If the place that the Moon is strong during the nativity, then the mother will have enough resources to bring her child to a higher level and help develop the child's mental abilities with a calm and peaceful way. The Moon is a nourishment and relaxing agent. It regulates the senses and the emotions , and grants people the capacity of taking care of areas of public relations, training administration, as well as the soothing (physician). The Moon symbolizes the queen, hoteliers financial institutions, public relations sailors, housekeepers, doctors nurses, midwives healers psychic abilities food establishments cooking, caterers, and other jobs that work directly with the public all over the world, and is the second significator for the wife. The Moon is a status symbol in the administration due to being the wife of the King. If she is strong, the native is not required to work to attain status, and it is a sign of affluence, receptivity creativity, sensitivity, memory, exemplary actions and good habits.

The Moon is a female planet. It is warm, damp, and soft, satvic, and its constitution is a mix of vata and the kapha. The Moon's beauty is royal. It is blessed with beautiful looks, a friendly speech and its personality is unpredictable and unstable. The Moon is unpredictable as it alters its position every day. Based on the luminosity of the Moon and its strength, a weak Moon has a thin body and the full Moon could give a large body if it's connected to the ascendant or its Lord in a significant way, but in the solitude. Its complexion is tawny , and it governs silver and white shades, the water element salty tastes and the sensation of taste, Mondays, the direction of northwest and the northwest direction, as well as silver, bronze and pearl, watery locations such as hotels, public spaces and hospitals, as well as ships.

The Moon is a symbol of the face, mind, and consciousness perception, emotions, tolerance and receptivity. It also represents intellect feminine sensitivity, sensuality and imagination, good memory fertility, general weakness emotional health, and functional health. It regulates the flow of fluids throughout the body, as well as the quality of lymph and blood glands, tonsils, stomach, breasts the lymphatic system, face lung and chest. It controls the left eye for males and ovariesas well as the menstrual cycle, the uterus, the generative organs, and the right eye for females. If it is weak in a child's nativity, in addition to mental issues, it can cause insomnia, sleep disorders and drowsiness, lung issues as well as mouth-related problems (including losing taste) as well as neurological problems, seizures, water retention anemia, blood disorders, swelling of the your spleen, conditions of the ovaries and the uterus and tuberculosis. Menstrual disorders and the person born is prone to frequent cold and cough and fever, as well as inability to eat general weakness, etc. This is a sign of hyper-sensitivity, excessive reaction or inability to communicate and have difficulty connecting with emotions. The Moon is also a significator for health and well-being. Moon is also a symbol for nourishment, sleep social, public behavior and change as well as travel, education, basic and comforts, emotional harmony and family, financial stability happiness in marriage, inheritance, earnings and gains as well as love and affection and peace of mind as well as grains, milk and liquids.

Mars (Mangala)

Mars is the supreme commander for all the planets. Mars is a symbol of courage, both mental as well as physical. Mars is a reference to positions in paramilitary and military forces, police, professions that require metals and fire as well as engineering, chemical surgeons, dentists, and executive positions. It is the governing force for gangsters, makers and executioners, athletes entrepreneurs, builders, designers firefighters, martial arts, firefighters mechanics, project erectors and mechanics.

Mars can also be the general symbol of younger brothers. This adds an extra strength to natives and is a source of determination and strength. The insufficiency of Mars is a sign of a man who is uncouth and is not able to benefit from the support and comforts of his younger brothers. If it is strong in the nativity it indicates a desire for action and passion, as well as ambition. physical power, goal-oriented energy strength to endure courage, bravery as well as heroism, competition and fighting spirit, vigor and vim.

Mars is male planet dry, fiery pitta, tamasic and dry. Its character is brutal aggressive, unrelenting, active and generous. Its temperament is brutal, violent and angry. Mars has a short stature, an imposing and well-built body, eyes with red and slim waist. The complexion of Mars is blood red, and it is the ruler of bright red hues as well as the fire element bitter taste perception of sight, Tuesdays, the direction of south red coral, copper areas near the fire, kitchens battlefields, areas for violent and aggressive sporting events football stadiums, and military structures.

Mars symbolizes bones marrow, the chest blood and digestive fire, bile the intestine, forehead, neck and muscular system. It also represents visual acuity sinews, nose, and the external organs that generate. If it is afflicted or weak or afflicted, it can cause inflammation, hyperheat and inability to withstand food, burns, wounds injuries, fractures piles, liver complaints skin rashes, ulcers and lacerations, surgeries, various acute ailments as well as fevers (particularly violent) epilepsy, mental abnormalities as well as cancerous tumors and tumors in the muscles of the body when in close proximity to Rahu dysentery, typhoid and cholera boils and pox, and many more. This symbolise anger, irritability and haste and impatience. It also signifies inconstancy, impatience, lack of motivation and determination, as well as an attitude of 'all-or-nothing. Mars is also a general symbol for strength, energy enemies army, accidents acute illnesses, aggressiveness, assets, unmovable properties and motivations, arguments and fights. explosives, guns, weapons general physical or technical capabilities, sports, and surgeries.

Mercury (Budha)

Mercury is the ruler over all the stars. It is the ruler of our speech and rational minds, the analytical abilities, sharp intelligence as well as the ability to discern and trust. The Mercury persona is one who is thought-provoking and expert in the field of mathematics. Mercury symbolizes positions of advisory, astrologers strategists, financial advisors engineering, business, and related fields, research scholars writers, editors, communicators accountants, bookkeepers attorneys, specialists in analytic works software engineers, auditors educators, intellectuals transporters, publishers, brokers, salesmen, traders authors, diplomats, etc., and is the universal significator for acquaintances. If it is you are strong in your nativity Mercury is a reliable communicater with intelligence, rationality and wit. dexterity, skill mental and verbal ability as well as shrewdness, good judgement, humor, and flexibility.

Mercury is an eunuch planet as well as a tri-dosha, rajasic and tri i.e. it's constitution is blend of pitta, vata and the kapha. Its character is royal, warm and friendly, while its personality is a bit volatile and flexible. Mercury has the most appealing appearance and is funny and a lover of laughter and jokes, when it is strong in the chart of the natal as the Lord of the rising. Attractive features, a well-proportioned body, huge eyes and witticism make up its significance. The appearance of Mercury is similar to the grass color and it governs Earth element. It also governs mixed or diverse tastes scent The Wednesdays, the north direction brass, emerald locations for sports, business transport, communication airports, post offices accounting offices, locations in which non-violent, public sporting events are played libraries, parks booksellers, public gatherings, and libraries.

Mercury is the lower portion of the abdomen, skin, brain, nervous system and urinary bladder. It also includes the gastric juice, bronchial tube digestion, intestines, mouth, lungs, tongue the hands, and arms. When weak, it causes psychic diseases, insomnia, nervous breakdown, epilepsy, skin diseases, impotence, loss of memory or speech, vertigo, deafness, asthma, diseases of respiratory canal, disorders of intestines, dyspepsia, etc., and denotes difficulty in thought and communication, timidity, low self-esteem, aloofness, amorality, expediency, over-intellectualization and poor discrimination. Because Mercury is often weak when its sub-periods are operating in any nativity, it causes tension in the life, a lack of confidence or indecisiveness and so on. that ultimately lead to poor choices. This is especially true when Mercury has a weak chart of birth and also in transit during the execution of its sub-periods. This can cause a person to become feel agitated and cause paralysis if closely with the Rahu and the Ketu axis, when both the ascendant as well as its Lord are weak or the sign of Virgo is on the ascendant.

Mercury is also a general symbol of consciousness, communication as well as eloquence, education and childhood and logic maternal uncles, power as well as respiratory functions, elementary and higher education and math, humor, wit and professional positions psychic ability in short journeys, speculation and papers, as well as books publishing, places to entertain.

Jupiter (Guru)

Jupiter is a god for all of the planets. Jupiter is the preceptor for the gods. Jupiter is portrayed as a judge, preceptor and is connected to the treasury. When it is in a strong position in the nativity period, it indicates the top positions in politics and administrative posts as the chairmen of industrial establishments financial advisors, contractors bankers, senior executive positions in the governments, kings, politicians as well as lawyers, bureaucrats doctors, pharmacists priests judges, teachers, Astrologers, management experts and administrators. It is also the governing force for propaganda of spirituality, cooperation with the government, education and law financial institutions, advisory positions, and is the principally a significator for the husband. If it is strong, it brings an expansion, growth and spiritual and humanistic outlook and symbolizes confidence, wisdom, faith generousity, geniality optimism, joviality, and the ability to judge. It grants intelligence and knowledge of the scriptures throughout its main and sub-periods.

It symbolizes an older brother spouse in female-only nativities the male progenitors, riches integrity, morality, friendship God's grace, and father all the good things in the world.

Jupiter is male-dominated, gentle cool, warm and warm. It is satvic, kapha and satvic. Its character is kind and generous. Its temperament is calm, gentle and warm-hearted. Jupiter provides a stunning and magnificent appearance, small brown locks, tawny eyesand a big body, when it is found robust in a birth and is the ruler of the ascendant or the god of the ascendant. Jupiter has a sharp mind and is blessed with the various disciplines of learning. The color of its complexion is tawny. it is the ruler of yellow hues as well as the elements of the ether (akasha) element sweet taste and hearing sense the Thursdays, the north-east direction, gold, yellow topaz, Treasury, vaults, banks, and other noble places like high-end courts, institutions altars, political assemblies and charitable institutions, as well as top banks, monastery and missionaries.

Jupiter is the symbol for the hips, fat tissue blood, the glands, arterial system the liver/gall bladder, the pancreas glands, digestion, hearing power and absorptive capacity, ears navel, feet, physical development, palate , and throat. If it is weak, it can cause congestion of the circulatory system, anemia, thrombosis jaundice, issues with the liver, such as ear infections dyspepsia, flatulence asthma, cough or phthisis, diabetes, and various other disorders of the pancreas glands. This is a sign of overconfidence and overindulgence. It also signifies excess and immorality. It also represents greed, immorality and a materialistic mindset (wanting to have everything you want). Jupiter is also a universal symbol for elder brothers, fathers sons, male progeny and teachers, as well as friends fortune, justice, education charity, wealth, simple gains, general fortune higher education, gains and income as well as mental inclinations to knowledge, happiness and wisdom. It also represents morality and virtue. It also signifies dharma, virtuous profession, wealth spirituality and spirituality, moral behavior, growth and compassion. It also indicates faith, honesty, sincerity common wisdom, divine grace, and, indeed all the good things in life.

Venus (Shukra)

Venus is a minister for all planets. She is the preceptor of demons. Venus is portrayed as a lover and preceptor. It is the one who governs life-saving drugs and the art, as well as vocations in the fields of finance, administration arts cinema, theatres painting design, music architecture Interior decorator, modelling advertising legal, teaching hotels, medicine and luxury objects and is the primary symbol of a happy wife or marriage. If it is it is strong in the nativity it is a signification of aesthetics of the world and its activities, psychic abilities and power, pleasures right behavior, elegance beauty, harmony the ability to think, creativity, rich tastes and affection, friendship and gentleness. charming, clarity, sociability harmony, balance elegant, grace and refined sensuality.

Venus is the female planet. It's warm, humid Rajasic, and its composition is a blend of vata and kapha. Its character is sensual, royal and generous, as well as benevolent. its personality is easygoing and tolerant. Venus is cheerful in spirit and is a petite body that is beautiful and has beautiful eyes, giving beautiful appearance, beautiful and sharp facial cuts, as well as the dark-bright, slightly curly hair that is found to be at a nativity. It governs the ascendant or is the Lord of ascendance. Its appearance is fair and it is ruled by royal blue, as well as variegated colors, the element of water and sour tastes and your sense of smell, Fridays, the direction of the southeast and diamonds locations of pleasure and entertainment, theaters and restaurants, cinemas rooms and art galleries, as well as theatres and symphony rooms, beauty salons, dance halls elegant clubs and shops.

Venus is the symbol of the pelvis and the sexual organs desire and desires, reproduction. It is the semen/ovum private organs, kidneys, face eyes, neck cheeks, chin, throat skin, venous system, etc. When it is weak, it triggers venereal diseases, disorders of the reproductive or urinary system such as diabetes, anemia, kidney stones cataracts and weakness of the sexual organs, mild paralysis asthma and phthisis. It also signifies cough, sexual perversions, cold and the inability to be sexually active and loss of body luster and more. It also signifies vanity, greed, laziness and ambiguity, as well as sentimentality, lack of charm sexual corruption, vice and a the lack of taste and sophistication. Venus is also a general symbol of vehicles, assets transportation, comforts luxury, dance, art and music, drama paintings and jewelry, love and family, marital tie as well as income and increases prosperity as well as wealth, materialistic pursuits, lavishness money, medical solvency and hypnosis, mantras, jewelry, perfumes and flowers and festivals, positions in the professional world such as musicians and singers, songwriters actors, dancers, actors, actresses and engineers, designers fashion designers and financial advisors, jewelers and perfumers, legal advisors ministers, teachers and ministers. It also represents people who deal with pleasure, entertainment and beauty, as and those who prefer to earn a living from the arts and romance, silver, exquisite foods, finery and ornaments poetry, advice, counsel, or fashion.

Saturn (Shani)

Saturn symbolizes servanthood on the world of planets. It is represented as a statesman or leader of the lower castes. It also represents jobs that require hard work and lower wages, management of workers, trying to get jobs in the government sector or labor-oriented industry routine workers and real estate agents, engineers and research workers and scientists, working with labor, working with fruit and roots as well as dealing with servants dealing with food that is spoiled stone or wood materials or butchers, dealing with activities or products beneath the earth, etc. If the nativity is strong represents the absolute perfection of humanity and its highest qualities spirituality, detachment, dedication, concentration, humility and integrity and sincerity. endurance, durability, leadership and discipline. It also represents responsibility as well as practicality, conservatism, realists, endurance, an attention to precision, sobriety and unwaveringness.

Saturn is an eunuch star that is cold dry, sluggish and worn out, vata and tamasic. The nature of Saturn is brutal self-centered and insolent, and its personality is hard and harsh. Saturn has a thin body, a long height and brown eyes with sunken ones and protruding teeth. It also has prominent wrinkles, lines long hands and a face, melancholy and lazy temperament, coarse and excessive hair, when it is strong in a nativity . Saturn is the ruler of the ascendant or the god in the ascendant. The color of Saturn is dark, and it is ruled by the black, navy blue and bright brown shades air elements as well as astringent flavor as well as the feeling of touch, Saturdays, the direction of the west iron, steel, blue sapphire, lead filthy places, slums and sewers garbage dumps underground cellars, basements, graves, mines, inaccessible areas such as hermitages, retreats, prisons, lonely and neglected or sad places cemeteries, abandoned buildings and ruin.

Saturn is the name given to the nerve tissue, muscles joints, tendons, teeth, spleen as well as the shin, which is a part of the leg between knee and ankle the gall bladder and phlegm, respiratory system, secretive system, and bones. If weak, it can cause pain and constant illness that can cause chronic and degenerative illnesses such as leg fractures cancer, tumors, diseases of glands, skin disorders and arthritis. It also symbolizes paralysis, the emaciation, gout, rheumatism as well as rickets, consume of flatulence, deformities body coldness nerve disorders, indigestion insanity, dyspepsia, numbness and windy conditions and impotence, senility for men. It also signifies pain asthma, and blockage of the bodily functions such as the retention of urine obstruction of the intestinal tract and intestinal obstruction. And it signifies anxiety, insecurities, isolation as well as depression, rigidity loneliness, stinginess and insanity fear, melancholy of slowness, austerity and a sense of worry insecurity, fear, miserliness and self-centeredness. Saturn is also a universal significator for endurance, challenges such as humiliation, suppression, falling (from the top or from a high point) and misdeeds, poverty and sorrow. anger, grief and authority figures, the form and design of buildings, steel, coal, wood delay, denial labor, elders land and property, management, death, sickness sadness and misery as well as renunciation, restraints on theft, thieves subordinates, servants construction workers, the leaders of the weak as well as low tech industry mass production morticians, farmers sweepers, gardeners, agricultural and menials. ascetics, monks, hermits who working with iron, metal steel, and leather products, services, slavery prison as well as loss, fate restriction, contraction and separation. It also signifies obstruction, prisons, asceticism, isolation uglyness, crime, and fear.

Rahu (Moon's north node)

Rahu is depicted as a diplomat as well as the shadowy planet. It is also an infamous deceiver when used favorably. It signifies diplomatic work, tasks that require manipulation of facts, and deals with the use of drugs and poisons. It is a sign of cheating and pleasure seekers, immoral and moral acts, speculative trading markets, etc.

It is a phlegmatic condition and causes malignant growth. If it's afflicted, it causes economic setbacks, malignant development and phlegm-related diseases as well as intestines, boils skin and spleen ulcers, blood pressure, worms etc. It can cause a smoky and unattractive appearance as a result of eating habits that lead to overeating. This results in unpleasant smells and a dirty nail and body.

Ketu (Moon's South Node)

It's hot and dry in the natural world. The condition causes injuries and inflammation, fevers, intestinal disorders, abnormalities as well as low blood pressure, hearing loss, speech problems and a sluggish body that has prominent veins. It is portrayed as a saint and draws people to more spirituality and mysticism.

## Chapter 2: Sun (Surya)

Sun is the source of the whole Solar System. It is the closest Star located approximately 93 million miles away from Earth. It is the most massive Celestial body within the Solar system and is nearly seven times the size of all the planets combined. Scientists have concluded that Sun does not have an actual solid mass, but it is made up of gaseous matter that are burning continuously and emitting enormous heat. All planets revolve around Sun as it's the main life source and only luminary in the real sense.

Mythological: Hindu Mythology Sun is considered as the son of Aditi and Sage Kashyap. Aditi was the mother of the Gods. The sons of her were defeated in battle by demons. Aditi asked sun to birth to her to be able to fight and defeat the demons so that Gods were able to repay their rightful due. Sun accepted the request to be born Aditya. As the source of the universe, all life, force and energy and the creator to Prana, Sun is worshipped as the Sun God and is held with esteem. Westerners refer to sun god Sun, Apollo. They believe that Apollo as the Sun as the child of Jupiter and Latona. Apollo is the younger brother to Diana and is revered by Greeks. Hindus consider that Sun is always moving through a chariot steered by seven horse. This could be due to the fact that Sun has all seven colors of the spectrum (VIBGYOR). There is a belief that Sun is able to travel all the way around Mount Meru everyday causing day and night.

The Astrological Meaning: Some of the most significant significance according to Uttara Kalamrita are:) Soul) Power or Strength) worship of Shiva d) Trees with thorns) Favor of the King or the ruler (f) Father G) awakening of wisdom or knowledge h) Bones) Eye J) The Bile) Acute or inflamed complaints) body m) timber n) Ornaments) Rulership over the eastern direction P) Copper Q) Rubies) Eastern face.) Face. It is commonly believed that weak Sun is a source of deficiency with regards to the above-mentioned signs and a powerful Sun is the source of numerous boons.

Other Astrological Aspects to Consider: Sun rules over the Leo sign. It is elevated at the 10th degree of Aries. He is ineffective or severely disabled in 10° Libra. Its Mooltrikona Rashi is in Leo starting at (0 20 to 20 degrees). It is extremely powerful during the day and is considered to be a royal among the planets. Its skin is red and the god of the presiding is Agni. Sun is a male planet, and belongs to Kshatriya

Varna. It is a symbol of the men of power and the class of warriors. Sun is a predominant Sattawik planet. It is a symbol of a strong taste. Sun is a honey-colored eyes, a square shape and is clean. He has good behavior, is powerful smart and manly, and has hair that is not as long around his face. Sun is in good terms with Moon, Mars and Jupiter and antagonistic towards Venus as well as Saturn. It is not averse to Mercury. Sun symbolizes one Ayana. The time between the time that Sun begins to enter Capricorn until the time that Sun leaves Gemini Rashi , the period is called Uttarayana. When Sun is in Cancer and continues until it leaves Sagittarius this period is called Dakshinayana. Sun is thought to be more powerful in the direction of southern.

Moon (Chandra)
It is the sole satellite orbiting the earth. While it is regarded as an astrological luminary, it doesn't emit light, however it shines because of the reflection of sun's radiation. At its perigee, moon's distance is 356404 Kilometres from earth, and at its apogee is 406680 Kilometres from earth. In the same way for all planets, its orbit is an elliptic. Moon is almost 1/4th of the size of Earth. It is interesting to note that only

one-half moon's light is visible to the human eye on Earth.

Mythology: According Harivansha Purana, moon was Sage's son Atri and was fostered by the Ten DISHAS (directions). Moon was married to his daughters Daksha Prajapati. They were the number 27. They are called the 27 Nakshatras that are part of the Zodiac. Moon visits each one for a day, rotating. He did however show Rohini who was one of 27th wives unjust favors. He also escaped with the wife from Brihaspati who was the Deva Guru. Daksh the father-in-law cursed Moon to be consumed and a slow decline. Mercury was born as a result of the interaction between Moon with Brihaspati's wife. Brihaspati.

In accordance with western concepts, Moon is regarded as the Mary, the Virgin Mary in the religion of Roman Catholics and nourishing mother of the heavens. She is also the queen of night, also known as Luna (Diana). Diana She is the sister to Apollo. She is responsible for chastity, as well in fertility.

Astrological Significance: As per Uttara Kalamrita, the following are some of the signs associated with the Moon as follows: a) Intelligence) Perfumes) Secret of ulcerous issues in the stomach) Woman E) sleeping a)

Joy g) Liquids) Malaria fever) Mother J) Pearls) Salt) Mind) Muhurta or 48 minutes duration) the worship of Gauri o) Cud Love p) Someone who performs penance or tapas) The strongest at night) eating food) Facial Lustre) Good Fruits) Fish and other aquatic creatures v) clothing.

It is evident that a full Moon will help with the above mentioned signs, while weak moons will result in some deficiencies.

Other Astrological considerations: Moon owns the cancer sign, but it is exalted at 3 degrees Taurus and is in severe debilitation at 3 degrees Scorpio. Its Moontrikona Rashi corresponds to Taurus. Moon can be described as the Karaka for mind and has a status of a royal among the planets. The color of its skin is dark and tawny. The sex of Moon is female. Moon symbolizes the commercial community or Vaishya. Moon represents Sattwika Gunas.

The Moon is extremely turbulent and phlegmatic. Her body is round and is a scholar. Her beautiful eyes and charming speech. She is fickle in her thinking and extremely attractive. She is the symbol of the one Muhurta i.e. an duration of 48 minutes. The flavor represented by the Moon can be described as Saline.

Moon is in good terms with Sun as well as Mercury and is neutral towards Mars, Jupiter, Venus and Saturn. Moon does not view any planet to be its enemy. But, Saturn, Mercury, Venus and Rahu and Ketu regard moon as their adversaries. Moon is strong in the northern direction.

Mars (Mangal)
Mars is among the planets that are outer. It is actually the closest planet to the Earth. The average distance of the Sun between the Sun and Mars is 140 million miles. Mars requires 687 days in order to circle the Sun. Mars has a smaller diameter than Earth, and its size is about 4,200 miles. It is about twice the size of the Moon. Its mass is around 1/10th of the mass of earth. Mars requires 24 hours, 37 mins and 23 seconds for its rotation around its axis. Mars looks like our Earth in a variety of ways, especially with regard to the time of rotation and tilt of its axis. This can make us believe like it's an escaped planet of Earth. The color for Mars appears red.

Mythology The following is a quote from Hindu Mythology Mars is considered as Bhumi - Putra. He is believed to be the father of mother Earth. According to legend, when the earth was submerged in vast sea. God Vishnu as the form of his Varaha avatar lifted earth, took it out and set it in a proper orbit. Mother Earth was grateful and requested a feminine blessing. O God grant me the gift of a child. In the extent that God was acquiescent. Mars was the outcome of that God-fearing union with the saved Earth. A story of this sort relates to Mars being the godson of the Lord Shiva and Mother Earth.

In the western astrology Mars is regarded as the God of war and hunting. In the Bible, Mars is represented by the Satan. Mars is the god of energy and force. Mars is regarded as the commander in Chief of celestial armies. Mars is the ruler of"the "Sama Veda"

Astrological Significance: The following are the signs of Mars according to Uttara Kalamrita A) Value (b) Land c) Strength) Battle) Foes) Archaeologist) Quadrupeds)"King I") Fire) the Bile) Wounds) Heat) Sword) Obstacles) The worship of Subrahmanya p) eating non-vegetarian food) The taste is bitter) The strength increases towards the evening s) Gold) The Man) Character) Painful urination) the blood) Desire) Anger) Snake

It is widely believed that an extremely robust Mars is a favorable performance in terms of the previously stated significations, whereas a weak Mars is a sign of a weakness

Other Astrological considerations: Mars own two signs specifically Aries as well as Scorpio. It is incredibly elevated at the 28 degree Capricorn, and severely debilitated at 28 ° Cancer. Its Mooltrikona Rashi is Aries. Mars is a symbol of power and holds the position that of the Commander in Chief within the Planetary Cabinet. His stature isn't excessive and is blood red in color; Kartikeya represents it. It is a masculine-oriented gender, with the predominant fire. It is a part of Kshatriya Varna with the predominant role that of Tamsik Gunas.

Mars is brutal and has blood red eyes and is a fickle-minded person generous, bilious, and has a slim waist and slim body. It symbolizes bone marrow. lives in the midst of fire. It is also the symbol of the time of day (Ahoratra i.e. it is a time period that spans from sunrise to the next). It is a symbol of bitter taste and it is strongest in the direction of the south. It is kind towards Sun, Moon and Jupiter. It is antagonistic towards Mercury as well as neutral towards Venus as well as Saturn.

Mercury (Buddha)
Mercury is located at an average 36 million kilometers away from the Sun. At the Apogee the distance is around 43 million miles, and at the perigee, it's around 29 million miles away from the Sun. It rotates around the Sun over

the course of 88 days. Its diameter is around 3200 miles. Because its size Mercury is extremely small and its mass small, its gravity pull is naturally fragile.

There is no atmosphere surrounding Mercury since it is near to the Sun. Additionally, one part of Mercury is extremely hot and its temperature is about 360 degrees Celsius; the other half is extremely cold, and much cooler than our Arctic region during extreme winter. The period of revolution and rotation is the same so only one portion of Mercury will be facing the Sun while the other will remain dark, even with temperatures lower than freezing.

Mythology Mercury came into existence because of the union between Moon with Tara who was the spouse of Brihaspati Brihaspati, the Deva Guru. The legend says that Moon took Tara and ate her refuse at The Ashram in Shukra. The Guru of Asuras. In the end, when all gods pleaded to the higher judgement of Moon but he realized his error. A remorseful moon returned Tara to Brihaspati. Tara had been carrying moon's baby. The baby was delivered. The baby was beautiful. Tara had revealed her father to Brihaspati who, in an Brahmanical acceptance gesture, took the inevitable.

In western astrology, Mercury is thought to be the child of Jupiter and Maia who is who is the child of Atlas. He is thought to be a friend to Apollo perhaps because Mercury is the closest star to the Sun.

Astrological Significance: A significant meanings of Mercury according to Uttara Kalamrita is listed below. A) education B) Treasury c) Mathematics d) Knowledge) speech f) Infantry) the writing) Green color I) Astrology and Astronomy) Commerce)"Eunuch") Skin) The worship to Vishnu the god of Vishnu) Atharva Vedas) Lover of the north-west direction) Highly well-versed in Puranas or epic epics major questions) Grammar) Maternal uncle) Yantras t) Very powerful tantrik u) Self-control) Devotion) Navel) Children y) Humility Z) powerful in the morning.

If Mercury is strong, a favorable result in the above signs will be observed and vice versa in the event that Mercury has a weak.

Other Astrological Concerns: Mercury rules over Gemini and Virgo signs. Mercury is highly exalted at 15 degrees Virgo and is severely debilitated around 15 degrees Pisces. This sign's Mooltrikona symbol is Virgo.

Mercury is the symbol of speech. In the planetary cabinet , it is considered to be an apparent heir. Its skin tone is comparable to

grass. The god of the presiding is Vishnu as well as also neuter. It is the symbol of Earth in the form of Panchbhootas. It is a symbol of Vaishya which is also known as the Commercial Community. It has the majority of Rajsik Gunas.
Mercury is a handsome man and is able to create puns or use words with double meanings and humour. Mercury is a mix of all three humours : Bile, Phlegm and wind. It is a symbol of the skin. It is found in the playground. It is a symbol of an individual Ritu (It is about two months duration). It is a symbol of mixed taste. It is a powerful symbol in the direction of the east. It is friendly with Sun as well as Venus. It is close to the Moon and neutral with Mars, Jupiter and Saturn. It is neutral both to Rahu as well as Ketu.

Jupiter (Guru)
Jupiter is far above the asteroids' swarm. It lies at a distance of around 500 million miles away from the Sun. It is the largest planet in the solar system. Its diameter is 88,000 miles, which is 10 times larger than the Earth. It takes just 12 or 13 years one time around the Sun.
Jupiter has a round shape. The upper portion of Jupiter isn't fully solidified. This means that the time of rotation across all regions of Jupiter is not even. The planet rotates extremely fast,

and can complete one full rotation in not more than 10 hours. Jupiter has 11 satellites unlike earth, which has just one Satellite and Mars has two.

Mythology Jupiter has been regarded as the Guru Devtas. He is the father Maharishi Angira. Maharishi's wife gained the knowledge and methods of doing the Vrata from Sanat Kumars in order to have the birth of a son. She performed the vrata in total devotion, as well as the Gods were happy and a child came into their home. Son was god of knowledge Jupiter.

The ancient Greeks think of Jupiter as the godfather of the Gods and gods. ZEUS. Egyptians refer to it as AMMON. It is also known as AMMON. Norse calls it the THOR. Babylonians call it MERODACH

Astrological Significance: A few of the most significant signs of Jupiter according to the Uttara Kalamrita are listed below. A) Brahmans) Teachers) Cows) treasure) A large or strong bodies f) Fame) Intelligence H) Astronomy and Astrology I) Sons J) Grand Sons) Older brother) The Indra) Precious stones) Dharma) yellow colors) Physical health) A clear and unambiguous view) facing towards north. The s) Mantra t) Holy holy water or sites that are sacred u) Intellect) Lord Brahma w) gold and high top quality Topaz) worship of Shiva The Lord Shiva) A solid understanding of the classical texts Z) Vedanta system of philosophy.

It is commonly believed that an extremely robust Jupiter is ideal for the above-mentioned signs, while the weak Jupiter has some deficiencies.

Other Astrological considerations: Jupiter owns two signs which are Sagittarius as well as Pisces. It is highly high within Cancer in 5 degrees, and severely debilitated at 5 ° Capricorn. The Mooltrikona sign of the sign is Sagittarius. Jupiter is the god of knowledge and happiness.

In the cabinet of the planet, it holds the post of minister. Its skin is dull and it has a tawny appearance. The god of the skies in Jupiter can be identified as Indra. It is masculine in gender. Its component includes Sky (Ether). It is part of Brahmin Varna and is primarily one of the Sattwika planet.

Jupiter is an enormous bodied individual and has eyes of honey colour and hair that is phlegmatic. It is intelligent and able to learn all Shastras. Jupiter represents fats within the body. It is located inside the room of treasure. It symbolizes a time period that lasts for a month. It symbolizes sweetness. It is potent to the west. It is kind with Sun, Moon and Mars. It is inimical with Mercury in the same way as

Venus and along with Saturn it is neutral. It is an ally to Rahu and is neutral to Ketu. Another interesting fact to be noticed is the fact that none of our planets regards Jupiter as a threat to its existence. But, Jupiter considers Venus and Mercury as its adversaries.

In the astrology field, there is no natural blessing other as Jupiter. The simple position in the constellation of Jupiter on Lagna as well as Kendra is believed to alleviate numerous afflictions that are associated with the Horoscope.

Venus (Shukra)

Venus is more close than the Sun than the Earth. So, at times Venus is located the space between Earth as well as the Sun. The average distance from sun is approximately 67 million miles. The difference is not that significant since Venus' orbit Venus is almost circular. Distance between Earth and Venus during the inferior conjunction period will be just 25,5 million miles. The dimension of Venus is similar to Earth. Venus has the size of 7,600 miles, while Earth has 7,900 miles in diameter. The sun revolves around it for about 225 days. The atmosphere layer surrounding Venus is dense, distinctive and captivating. The luminosity of Venus is due to the reflection power that its surrounding atmosphere has. For earth-based observers Venus is not more than 48 degrees to the Sun.

Mythology Shukracharya is the child of Sage Bhrigu. He is the preceptor of demons. Shukra is the sole one who was worthy of an understanding of Mrit the Sanjivani Vidya, by the Lord Shiva. This knowledge is said to bring even dead people back to the world of.
Venus is regarded as the Goddess of love marriage, beauty, marriage and pleasures. It is a incarnation of Maha Lakshmi, who is the wife of Lord Vishnu. Venus is the ruler of her responsibilities in the Yajur Veda and the Vasant Ritu (April and May). According to western theology, Venus is also known to be Lucifer and Hebrews identified it as Astoreth..
Astrological Signification the Uttara Kalamrita gives the following meaning of Venus. A) Good clothing b) wedding c) income d) woman e) Brahmins) wife g) Joy from sexuality (h) flowers I) Conveyance) The silver) affectionate of south-east l) Cough) Rajsik nature n) Pearls) Happiness (p) having many females) Being honest r) Semen) dances) Afraid of worshiping Gauri and Laxmi the u) Mother to those born during the day) Genital organs with) Urinary tract ounce tract) Sturdy in the afternoon) Musical

instruments that are pleasant Z) skilled in the fine arts.

It is evident that the presence of a robust Venus produces excellent results in an Horoscope. However an insufficient Venus could cause some deficiencies in relation to the above signs. Other Astrological considerations: Venus owns two signs specifically Taurus in addition to Libra. It is incredibly exalted at 27 degrees within the Pisces rashi. The Mooltrikona of the natal sign is Libra. Venus governs semen (potency).

In the Cabinet of the planetary system Venus serves as a Minister alongside Jupiter. The color of Venus is varied. As per "Brihat Parashara Hora Shastra" the god that it is a representation of has the name Shachi (Consort to the Lord Indra). It is feminine in gender. It symbolizes water among the Panchbhootas. It is part of Brahmin Varna, and is a major part of Rajsik Gunas.

Venus is charming, happy in appearance, beautiful eyes and dazzling eyes. She is a poet. She is windy and phlegmatic. She also is curly in her hair. Venus is a symbol of a fortnight, which is a Paksha of the Moon. It is particularly strong in the direction of the north. It is associated with an acidic flavor.

It is very friendly to Mercury in particular and Saturn. It is inimical towards Sun, Moon, and Mars. It views Jupiter as neutral.

Saturn (Shani)
Saturn can be found 886 miles to the Sun. Saturn is less than Jupiter and has a diameter of 75,000 miles. It has nine satellites that are known to exist. It is volume-wise 700 times larger than earth. Its mass is less than 100 times the size of earth. Saturn is able to take 29 1/2 years to circle the sun. Therefore, on average it is in one rashi for a time between 2 and 2 1/2 decades.
Saturn is enclosed by a set of 3 concentric rings. The rings are distinct, and there is no empty space between the two rings. Saturn appears to be an blue ball, with three yellow rings.

Mythology Saturn was the father of Sun and Chhaya. Saturn is an astrological planet that has been a lot, mistreated and cursed by his wife and mother, the celestial Parvati. In actual fact, upon recognizing her mistake, Maa Parvati blessed to Saturn that any significant incident within the lifetime of an individual can be able to occur until Saturn accords his divine sanctity and sanctity to the work, either through an aspect or transit to the important house.

He is the older brother of Yama so he is an important role in the life of Yama and may bring about the end of life. So, if a negative dasa is in the air and simultaneously there is a bad movement that is associated with Saturn and the time of death has arrived, Saturn is certain to end the life of the person. However, Saturn also symbolizes detachment. It is a significant symbol of spirituality. There is no saint who can be born without a solid and well-placed Saturn.

Astrological Significance: As per Uttara Kalamrita, the following are the signs that represent Saturn. A) Infirmity b) Obstructions) Disease) rivalry e) sadness) Death) The maid servant) Assesses l) Outcasts) Longevity) Eunuch) The wind) Old age) Dirty cloth) The colour black) A significator of the father for those born in the night .) Shudras) Brahmin having Tamsik qualities s) Hair that is ugly) The worship of Yama U) Eyes downwards) telling lies) Thieves and hardheartedness and x) oil y) Hunter Z) Lameness

It is evident that strong Saturn can produce good results but in the event that Saturn is weak, it can create deficiencies in relation to the above-mentioned significances.

Other Astrological Thoughts: Saturn owns two signs which are Capricorn as well as Aquarius. It is highly exalted to 20 ° in the Libra Rashi and is handicapped around 20° in the Aries Rashi. Its Mooltrikona Rashi is Aquarius. It is believed to be to be the Karaka for the grief.

In the cabinet of the planets, Saturn is the symbol for servants. It has a dark-colored complexion. It is of a neutral gender. It is a symbol of Air in the Panchbhootas. It is part of Shudra Varna and has predominance of Tamsik Gunas.

Saturn is an obese and long body with honey-colored eyes. is temperamentally windy and has large teeth. is indolentand lazy, and has rough and coarse hair. Saturn symbolizes one year.

It signifies a strong taste. It is particularly strong in the direction of western. It is good with Mercury as well as Venus. It is antagonistic with Sun, Moon and Mars. It believes Jupiter as neutral. Rahu and Ketu both see Saturn as a friend.

Rahu and Ketu

Rahu and Ketu are considered to be Grahas in Vedic Astrology. They are not physical entities and are merely mathematically calculated areas that exert immense influence over the earth's inhabitants.

Moon in its orbit with a northerly path between South to North it traverses the ecliptic (the apparent path of the Sun). This intersection point is called Rahu or Dragon's head. At 180 degrees from the point Moon along its course to the south traverses the ecliptic. This is known as the dragon's tail, or Ketu.

Rahu as well as Ketu are the only two that are part of our system of astrology or. The reason why so much emphasis on the point at which the crossing between the ecliptic is explained must be comprehended. Since Sun is our body, and Moon can be thought of as the head,, the intersection is sure to produce an immense impact.

Rahu and Ketu aren't stationary in space , but they have a mean speed of around 20 degrees, and 30 mins one year. It takes 18 years and six months to create a complete circle around the Earth. The motion is retrograde. There is a concept known as Mean Rahu and True Rahu. In Hindu Astrology, we consider the real place in the astrological cycle of Rahu as well as Ketu.

Mythology: This tale relates to the huge churning the ocean by Devas along with the Asuras to snatch out Amrita. Lord Vishnu with the intent to preserve goodness made it a priority that Amrita should not be taken to the Asuras. To make sure of this, he assumed in the shape of Mohini. Mohini manipulated the seating arrangement so that she reached her

Devtas first. The Asura who was able to grasp the technique was Swarbhanu. He assumed the form of Devas and then positioned himself the middle of Sun as well as Moon. At the time of his term and he was also given Amrita from the deceived Lord Vishnu. In the beginning, before Swarbhanu was able to drink Amrita, Sun and Moon recognized the amrita. Lord Vishnu cut off his head by using his Sudarshan Chakra. But, a few drops of Amrita fell down, and the body and head were immortalized. The head symbolizes Rahu and the Tail refers to Ketu.

The head that was severed was taken from Simihika who was the mom of Asura Swarbhanu. She nursed it with patience. The head, over a long period of time was able to acquire the body of a Serpent and was later called Rahu. A Brahmin known as Mini adopted the body. He raised this body as his son. For this body, Lord Vishnu gave the head of a serpent. The result was Ketu who, over the course of time was an extremely revered and saintly seer. Rahu and Ketu are not pitying Sun as well as Moon for their actions in exposing them, and causing Eclipse. Astrological significance:

Rahu: Rahu is the personification of the following things as per Uttara Kalamrita. 1.) False Logic) Disruptive speech) Outcaste) an unreligious individual e) traveling to a foreign land f) Unclean g) Bones) abdomen ulcers) Falsehood) The direction of South Western K) serpents) Old age) Maternal grandfather) the worship of Vana Durga O) Writers Urdu as well as Persian or Persian) Breathing Q) Duodenal pain that is acute.

It is noted that robust Rahu is great for the above-mentioned signs, while a weak Rahu is the exact opposite.

Ketu: Ketu is the symbol for the following according to Uttara Kalamrita A) The worship of Chandi, Ganesh and others b) Medical practitioner) Vultures) Emancipation final e) Consumption) Fevers that cause pain) Bathing bathe in Ganges (h) The Great Penance) Wind complaints) Mantra Shastra k) Instability of the mind) diseases of the stomach and eyes Eye and stomach) Vedanta n) Grandfather O) Small boils or pox p) A friend of Shiva Q) Connection with foreigners or Shudras.

It is believed that a powerful Ketu generally produces good results while a malefic Ketu causes a lot of obstacles in the world of life.

Other Astrological Considerations:

Rahu: Rahu is in his own home within Virgo Rashi. Rahu is elevated when it is put in Taurus Rashi while it is weak when it is it is placed into Scorpio Rashi. There are a variety of opinions on this. Certain authorities consider exaltation points and Debilitation points to be Gemini and Sagittarius as well. There is a belief that Rahu produces yogkaraka results when placed in the Cancer Rashi. But, it must be noted that since it is an Chaya Grah it gives results that are based on the influence of planets. It is widely believed that when it is Benefic or Benefic influence it can give a excellent results. It is typically thought of as a planet that is suitable for comforts in the world. But, there are a lot of Maya connected to Rahu. Today, Rahu symbolizes Computers and Mass Media.

Rahu is in good terms with Jupiter, Venus and Saturn. Rahu views Sun as well as Moon as enemies and with regard to Mercury it is neutral.

Ketu: Ketu is exalted when it is placed within Scorpio rashi as well as debilitated when it is placed on the Taurus Rashi. Certain authorities have listed the Debilitation and Exaltation points to be Sagittarius and Gemini as well. It must be noted it is Ketu is more oriented towards the spiritual side and represents the Karaka for emancipation at the end of the tunnel, while Rahu is more focused on worldly pleasures. It is also to be noted it is Chaya Grah is essentially achieving results. Chaya Grah gives results according to the associations.

Ketu is in good terms with Mars, Venus and Saturn. It regards Sun as well as Moon as his adversaries and in the direction of Mercury as well. Jupiter it is neutral.

## Chapter 3: Twelve Houses And Their Meanings

1st House

The 1st house is the representation of the person who is his natural nature and the state of vitality, health and longevity. It also represents happiness and appearance. well-being, general state of mind to life, reputation and status, wishes and their fulfillment as well as the body's parts, including appearance and the head (cranium as well as forehead) and the brain pituitary glands, hair and pituitary glands. In the case of weakness, the first house or of illnesses that affect either the house itself or to its Lord results in a weakened constitution, leading to mental tension, headaches and paralysis, giddiness injuries, scars, irregular hormone activity, mental illness and brain fever, stuttering and nose bleeding. A healthy Sun and Mars as a symbol of energy and vitality can serve as protection.

2nd House

2nd house is a symbol of wealth family, livelihood food, male child higher education, professional status as well as spouse second marriage, continuation of marriage and possession of precious stones and precious metals and cash. It also represents earning capacity financial status wealth, fortune and movable properties, speech vision, and the organs of the body - the face as well as its bodily organs (nose mouth, throat teeth, eyes and mouth especially the right) facial bones upper neck , its bones, gullet larynx cerebellum, trachea cervical region, tonsils, cervical bones, and tonsils. In particular, the weakening the second house or afflictions related to it or the lord result in an increased risk of digestive problems or speech disorders. the cervical, throat gums, eyes teeth dental, gums, eyes. And, most importantly, diseases caused by weak venous systems. The strong Mercury as a significator for speech, serves as a protection cover.

## 3rd House

The 3rd house symbolizes younger siblings or brothers neighbors, physical strength, courage athletics ingenuity, entrepreneurialism and the ability to understand (learning) communication, brief journeys, the beginning of spiritual practices, writing and communicating capabilities and body's components - the neck, lower shoulder, arms, the ears (especially ears that are right) and shoulders, hands and collar bones thyroid gland and the nervous system, as well as respiratory systems, etc. For instance, weakness in the third house or afflictions related to it or the lord result in the risk of problems with the respiratory canal, conditions that affect thyroid glands, imbalances within your nervous system. Depression that results in stammering, partial paralysis shoulders, shoulder pains, fractures in the region of the collar bone and partial deafness. They also suffer from asthma, respiratory disorders tuberculosis, and so on. The strength of Mercury as a symbol of communication, serves to provide a protective shield.

Third house: The 3rd is a an extremely important and assists the person who is born there in his studies and professional. The third house is akin to Mercury and Sun since it houses knowing and confidence, as well as writing, communication, and marketing. The house is a symbol of many meanings and plays the role of an advisor and leader.

4th House

The 4th house is associated with mother happiness, joy, education family and friends, supporters, the basics of education, conveyances and vehicles domestic peace, peace of mind, mental peace spirituality (ATMA) trust, righteous conduct closure to home, comforts, luxurious lifestyles, birthplace country and immovable property such as real estate, land tanks, wells house, home assets, the body's parts, including your ribs, the heart and lungs, chest and breasts. In particular, weakness of the fourth house and/or ailments of the fourth or its Lord can lead to an increased risk of coronary disease and physical conditions of the chest, breasts, and epigastria region, lung diseases, mental disorders, lunacy , and issues related to the circulatory systems. A powerful Moon as a symbol of motherhood, Venus as significator of comfort and Mars as a significator for permanent properties act to provide a shield of protection.

Fourth house represents the anchor sheet of the life of people who are native, as the fourth house is dynamic in its configurations. When a child is born, it controls particularly the joy of the mother. In the early years, it governs education. As you enter the adult phase in life, the ego governs assets marriage, vehicle, and the comforts of life. If strong, it can provide the longest-lived parents. Its Lord is thought to be the most benefic planet , and it is believed to be the most beneficent house.

5th House

5th house is a symbol of emotional intelligence, intelligence discernment and discrimination mental and intellectual abilities memory, creativity emotional happiness romantic love and love, as well as potential gains from investments, organizational abilities Progeny, success children, knowledge of wisdom, higher education/education and training, a fall from the position, social life desires spiritual pursuits, students and students, devotion mantras, yantras and amulets, merits and resources that we can bring into our lives as well as the future, digestion etc. and body's parts: stomach, upper belly, gall bladder, liver the spleen, the pancreas, colon diaphragm, the spine, the spinal cord, pregnancy and so on. In particular, the weakness of the fifth house or afflictions related to it or the lord can lead to the risk of developing diabetes, peptic ulcers colic pains, anemia, gall bladder stones acidity, spinal issues, dyspepsia, diarrhea and pleurisy, heart issues and so on. A healthy Sun as a symbol of digestion and a an nutrient for the body, serves as a protection cover.

6th House

The 6th house is associated with accidents, disputes, and diseases as well as enemies, debts adversaries, rivals fear, thieves worry, doubts, weaknesses, vices, solid financial situation mother uncles, services employees, health and protection from losses caused by theft, fire and fraud conflict, miscommunications with litigation, and the body parts like the waist navel, lower abdominal kidneys, small intestine the upper portion of the large intestinal tract, function of the appendix, etc. For instance, weakness of the sixth house or afflictions with respect to its Lord or sixth house result in the possibility of problems with appendicitis as well as colic, poisoning constipation, hernias and blood urea, mental disorders exhaustion, as well as nervous breakdown. This means that the health, financial situation as well as the position in relation to your opponents is reflected by this house. A healthy Mercury and Mars as indicators of health, act to provide a shield of protection.

7th House

The 7th house is associated with long-term relationships such as legal ties, spouses or partners in life as well as partners in business. It represents fertility, vitality as well as passion, sexuality moral behavior, pleasures, comforts and living in foreign countries as well as the success of love affairs conjugal life, living at traveling, home or business expansion and body components - pelvic and girdle the bladder, lumbar region lower part of the large intestinal tract, internal sexual organs, such as the uterus, ovaries, cervix and testicles, prostate gland, among others. For instance, weakness of the seventh house and/or ailments related to its Lord or the Seventh House can cause an increased risk of developing organs such as arthritis, venereal diseases Gout issues, pains in the urn as well as impotence, sterilization kidney problems, etc. A solid Venus as a significator of marriage, can act to provide a shield.

## 8th House

The 8th house is associated with the longevity of life, as well as research and interest in the occult, mystical sciences, MOKSHA, outer and inner changes, both past and future events including succession, deaths, last will and testamentary, financial arrangements easy gains, marital tie, danger, fear and obstacles such as litigation bankruptcy, theft loss, disgrace, misfortunes and disappointments, as well as the body's organs, scrotum as well as anus, the sexual organs of the outside and organs of excretory pelvic bones. For instance, weakness of the eighth house and/or ailments towards the energy of this house, or their lord causes the possibility of fissures, hydroceles, impotence pimples, urinary infections as well as boils, chronic ailments and so on. A powerful Saturn as a symbol of longevity, acts by providing a protection cover.

## 9th House

The 9th house is associated with father spiritual teacher, preceptor instinctual inclinations and spiritual development duty, charity, virtue and destiny based on the experience of the past and its resulting happiness and peace, meditation, travel abroad lengthy journeys of a short duration and living in other countries, education abroad grace, luck general fortune, abrupt and unexpected results, religion and pilgrimages, philosophy, laws, medicines remedies, past,. and body's parts, thighs, the left leg and thigh bone the bone marrow of the hips, their joints, as well as an arterial system. For instance, weakness in the ninth house or afflictions of the 9th house, or their lord result in vulnerability to anemia, lower production in blood supply, thalassemia the leukemia virus, fevers that are high arthritis, diabetes and problems in the thighs and hips, and so on. A powerful Jupiter as a significator of general luck as well as a powerful Sun as a symbol of fathers, can be used as an effective cover for protection.

## 10th House

The 10th house is associated with profession or career and promotion. It also represents power, livelihood fame and public esteem. It also represents standing, position honor, karma in life and character authorities, authority, government employer, living abroad future birth, happiness due to masculine progeny and debts, and the body's parts, such as knees and kneecaps, bone and joints. For instance, weakness in the tenth house or afflictions to the tenth house , or its lord, result in arthritis, knee injuries and joints, joint inflammation general weaknessand skin disorders and allergies, an overly swollen body, and so on, in addition to having a negative impact on professional issues. A healthy Sun as a symbol of organization, can act in the protection of.

11th House

The 11th house symbolizes the income, prosperity, gains profits, friends older siblings, dreams and aspirations , their fulfillment as well as their fulfillment. The body's components - shanks ankles, the shin bone left ear, right leg and the arm of left. For example, weakness in the eleventh house, or ailments of the 11th or its Lord can cause an increased risk of developing circulatory problems as well as fractures in the lower leg and pain in the legs, issues with low production of blood, cancers of the leg and limbs, etc. A powerful Saturn as a symbol of simple sources of income can act as a shield.

12th House

The 12th house is associated with expenditures, losses, expenses for charity, ending in life or exile living in other countries, obstacles in the life of a person, separation from loved ones, straying or retreating, the enlightenment process, transcendence, seclusion prison, hospitalization the comforts of bed, a peaceful sleep , and working behind the scenes, for example, working in a hospital, asylum prison, military quarters or a monastery and so on. and also the body's parts, including eyes, lymphatic system, as well as feet. In particular, the weaknesses in the twelfth place or afflictions to the 12th home or the lord of it can result in issues for the body parts that are governed by the house. It can cause insomnia and weaken the immunity power. A powerful Moon is a significator of immunity and peace of mind and peace, as well as a strong Venus as a significator of happiness in the marriage and comfort, act to protect. Planets in the 12th house can encourage you to travel to far-off lands or locations.


6. ASCENDANT (Lagna)
Rising Sign often referred to as an Ascendant could be an Ascendant, or Rising Sign. It is the Zodiac Sign that was rising on the eastern horizon during the time when the native was birth was. It is often abbreviated on the birth chart as AS or AS. If you know the date you were born as an Ascendant, your birth date can be calculated according to the exact degree.

There is a belief that when the Ascendant moves closer to the start of the Sign and the more intense the results will become evident by the person. It is also believed to be the case if the Sun is located in a weak area of your birth chart (such for instance, if the person was born in the night). It is also believed to be more weakened when a person is born near the end of the Sign's Ascendancy shortly ahead of the moment when the new Sign is born.

Since it is the case that Ascendant Sign is unique to the date and time of birth of the person and represents the surroundings and the environment that a person could be influenced by in their early years and is regarded equally important and important like the Sun as well as Moon Signs because the other aspects on the chart are affected by this Sign.

The Ascendant is believed to be the face you wear when in public. It creates the initial impression we give when we meet people for the first time. In most cases, if you're in awe of how others describe you it's because they're describing your personality in this way. The Ascendant is a part of your appearance and character and even having an impact on your physical appearance at times. The Sign is expressed in your appearance, style and mannerisms. It also shows in the way you behave. Astrologers believe that the Sign gets weaker once an individual reaches the age of 30 of age, when their confidence in themselves increases. they are.

Since the Earth has 24 hours to rotate around its axis. All 12 signs of the zodiac will be rising up on the eastern sky. In a single day, there will be twelve Lagnas. So 24 hours divided by 12 = 2 hours. This is the time period for each Lagna.

Each sign is 30 degrees. So 2 hours equals 120 minutes multiplied by 30 degrees equals 4. Thus every 4 minutes, the Lagna grows by one degree.

The dates and hours I'm referring to are rough round off figures. There could be slight fractional variances based on the time of year and location, etc.

Thus, if the baby was born at kolkata within 1 hours, i.e. around 7.39 The Ascendant would rise by 60minutes multiplied into 4 equals 15°. Therefore, in 7.39 it will rise to 15° Capricorn. If he was born two hours after sunrise then the Earth will have spun further as well the sign of Capricorn would have moved upwards and the zodiac sign Aquarius will be rising above easterly horizon. Therefore, at 8.40 the baby born in kolkata will be born with Ascendant one degree of Aquarius.

Instead of the 15th of January, imagine that the baby is born on 30th January in the same location in Kolkata, in the exact same hour 6.39 AM. The 15th of January Sun was at one degree Capricorn and, since it moves at 1-degree per day the 30th of Jan Sun will be at fifteen degrees Capricorn. Therefore, the child's Lagna in this instance will be 15 degrees Capricorn.

In a rough sense the most important rule is that if you were born in Sunrise the time of the Ascendant is the exactly the same as the sign under the sign in which Sun is located and Lagna degree (Longitude) are the same in the same way as Suns degrees. If your birth occurs earlier or prior to Sunrise then increase or decrease the degrees by 1 degree every 4 minutes.

If the birthplace changes the longitude and latitude can also change. Sometimes, the time zone changes too, and the Sunrise time is also altered accordingly. This is why ascendant changes from place the next.

Before the advent of computers, when calculations were done manually using the Ephemeris used to show the Sidereal time at noon 12.00 for all days of the week. By taking this sidereal time, with the aid of a Table of Ascendants that was used to provide an illustration of the various variations of the

Lagna for different locations on Earth and time-related differences. ascendant calculations were calculated.

It is currently in the country of many. Since it is an artificial advance of one hour in time and has no impact on Suns movement. Therefore, if you were born during the time that daylight savings time in effect then we must take the local time plus 1 hour, which is the real time.

## 7. JANMA Rashi(Moon sign)

Janma Rashi (moon sign) in astrology refers to the Rashi also known as the sign that Moon is in the moment of birth. It is a significant factor in the prediction of the day-to-day life of a person. The moon sign horoscope is created and can have a significant influence on the day to day activities. The three charts used in order to assess the power of planets include the ascendant chart and birth chart. Rashi chart, and chart.

As we all know, among the seven worlds that the planet Moon is one of them. Moon is one of the most swiftly moving.. Daily and weekly predictions are made by analyzing the Birth Rashi chart.

When compared to regular routine, if the chart of Ascendant is the final report card, then your birth Rashi chart serves as the monthly report card. Therefore, in order to anticipate anything on the report card, monthly reports on the exam are important.

Let's discuss these 12 Rashas that occur when Moon is in various signs:

Aries

The birth Rashi Lord is Mars. Aries Sign is considered to be a moveable sign. Aries is ruled by Mars possess a certain amount of independently thinking, reasoning and thinking. Birth moon in Aries suggests being reckless adventurous, ambitious and entrepreneurial. Moon in Aries can make the native impulsive.

Taurus

Taurus is the sign of Venus. Moon is in Taurus is elevated meaning that Moon has every resource available to accomplish its main goals. The native is influential as well as commanding, and make great leaps in their lives. Moon in Taurus is a sign of a liberal native, content throughout middle and old older. They are lively, unique and adaptable.

Gemini

Gemini sign is the ruling sign of Mercury. Mercury is an astronomical planet that is neither female nor male. The planet is earthy dual signed planet , and can range between malefic and benefic based upon its relationship with a malefic planet. Moon in Gemini symbolizes creativity, affection for women, persuasiveness curly hair, and inclination toward studying the Scriptures.

Cancer
The birth of Rashi to be a Cancer sign is believed to be the luckiest sign. It is controlled by the Moon. It is a moveable sign. Moon located in Cancer signifies charming character that is wealthy, and in the influence of women and many unprofitable and lucrative trips. Natives are extremely cautious, sensitive, thrifty and traditional.

Leo
Leo birth Rashi is under the rule of the Sun. It is an unchangeable sign. The Sun is male-dominated planet. It's fiery and peach-colored. Natives will sport a striking look and appear to be blonde. They have big cheeks and large faces. Leos could be prone to colic problems They are also likely to be unsatisfied, liberal as well as generous, confident, proud and aristocratic.

Virgo
Aside from Gemini, Virgo sign is also controlled by Mercury. It is a dual earthy sign with a direction of south. People that are blessed with Moon in Virgo are blessed with beautiful skin and shoulders that are sunken, as well as a soft

body, and sweet voice. The native is kind and phlegmatic. They are conceited in self-esteem, a conservatism, sociable, and attracted to occult science and may be a popular Astrologer. The native also excels in performing arts such as dancing and music.

Libra

It is controlled by Venus as a male symbol. The sign is airy that is moveable in the natural world. Indigenous people are both holy and knowledgeable. They are thin, tall and intelligent. They are wealthy friendly, ambitious, and are awed by art.

Scorpio

It is controlled by Mars and is the feminine sign of Mars. This is an ethereal sign that is permanent in the natural world. Moon in Scorpio is a weak Moon therefore, people who are born under this Moon signify big eyes, large chests, round shanks and legs. Moon in Scorpio can also mean that the natives are straight and flexible, unhappy rich, impetuous and inflexible.

Sagittarius

It is the sign of Jupiter. Jupiter is male-oriented sign. It is a dual-natured sign and is the sign of fire. Birth Rashi Sagittarius is a symbol of broad face large teeth, indistinct shoulders as well as disfigured nails and arms. Natives possess a deep and creative minds, possess excellent speech, and are literary and arts lovers and are awe-inspiring in their ceremonies. They possess a reflective mind and a positive inheritance.

## Capricorn

It is the sign of Saturn and is an astrological sign that is feminine. It has a movable nature as well as being earthy. People that are born to Moon within Capricorn are kind and quick to perceive as well as active, smart and sagacious. They are also strategic untrustworthy and unpredictable.

## Aquarius

The sign of the water bearer is controlled by Saturn and is masculine and rooted in the natural world. Natives born under the sign of Rashi are beautiful and pure-minded, sensual diplomatic, artistic lonely, and bizarre. They are well-built with a body, big teeth, a slim belly, and youthful appearance.

## Pisces

Pisces is a watery sign that is controlled by Jupiter. The sign of feminine is dual in nature. Birth Rashi Pisces symbolizes a the long nose and a bright body. They're subordinate to males of opposite genders and are attractive, knowledgeable and curious. They develop a spiritual inclination towards the end of their life.

## 8. Introduction to birth chart

In addition to illustrating the possible placements of different planets at the time of birth; it also indicates the degrees of ascending on the eastern horizon. Utilizing the birth date and year, as well as the exact location of the birthplace and its longitudinal intersections, the birth chart or natal chart is constructed. The signification of a native's ascendance is referred to as the lagna. The lordship for the indicated sign can be determined by its degree of ascendance at a particular cusp.

The date and place of the birthplace of a native and the place of his birth and its coordinates play a major role in determining the planet's positions. The ascendant sign moon rise, sun rise of that particular day are also considered. One must consider the planets' positions for that specific day, which are described in almanacs. The Natal chart is the foundation of many astrological predictions since calculations are made regarding the location of the six planets that range from Sun to Saturn as well as moon phases for Rahu as well as Ketu.

The planets as per Indian Astrology are believed to block twelve signs. The sign that Moon is situated is called the birth sign, or Janam Rashi. The star constellation within which the moon is located is known as "Janam Nakshatra". The nine planets that have connection to particular aspects of our lives are the various aspects or bhavas in the chart of birth. There are two houses in the chart. Sun and Moon have one house each , while the other planets share heir the lordships, which have two houses. The placement of a planet on a particular Natal chart is determined by the longitudinal intersection of the planet and the intersection on the cusp.

The planets that are located in various signs represent the characteristics that are inherent, character and potentialities within us. A planet in exaltation signifies that the energy level at an exact degree is in line with the energy of nature contained in the planet in question.

## Chapter 4: How To Cast The Birth Chart

Before you learn about the other aspects of astrology you should now know the way a horoscope is created and how it is read. This article is not about the intricate maths involved in calculating lagna, planets, and planetary positions. Nowadays, even Astrologers use computerized software. From a practical perspective of understanding the fundamentals, you simply have to understand how birth charts are made and the best way to read and comprehend it.

The horoscope is a picture of the sky at the date of one's birth. It also shows where signs or rashis the 9 planets are located. It also illustrates another vital aspect of astrology, the Lagna or the Ascendant. It plays an important role in the analysis of a person's life. The ascendant is determined based on the time and place of birth. It varies from one place to another. This is due to the differences in latitude and longitude as well as the time of sunrise. Lagna is the name given to your own 1st house. It is important to note that your lagna can be located within one of 12 rashis. The counting of your personal houses is always done using the lagna. The details of the significance of the houses and the role they play in the following lesson.

The location of the planets at any given moment and time is calculated using the ephemeris or Panchang and the horoscopes created according to the Panchang. It's not some sort of mystic charting planet names on charts.

The planetary positions are measured differently. positions - Vedic as opposed to. Western astrology

Vedic Astrology is based on it's Niryana which is also known as the Sidereal Zodiac, where in the West, Astrology is based on the Sayana or the tropical zodiac. It's a very complex Astronomical topic. In short, the basic concepts will be as following.

The location and particularly the degree of the planets on an individual's birth chart drawn in accordance with western Astrology differ significantly in comparison to the chart created in accordance with Indian astrology. In accordance with the west sun sign Sun goes into Aries on the 21st day of March. However, as per our calculation, it is in Aries around the 14th day of April. There is therefore a difference of 24 degree difference. It is the Western also known as Sayana zodiac system computes calculations and forecasts based on the current position of the planets, from a zodiacal perspective of perspective. The system we use is known as Nirayana or the Indian System. Within the Nirayana System, planet's positions are observed from Earth by taking into consideration the tilt that occurs at the North Pole by making corrections to compensate for tilt.

If you use the conventional globe that is available and place it on your table, you'll see you can see that both North and South poles aren't at 90 degrees vertically but they are inclined. The tilt is around 23degrees east, and can greatly affect calculations in astronomy. Check out the image.

The reason for this inclination is by the shift of the vernal point, that is caused by the West to East rotation of the earth's axis. When playing table tennis, when you provide a spin that is sideways to the ball, it does is not just spinning according to the direction it is spinning, but it also swerves and swings through the air. As the earth spins towards the east along its axis and as well, the North Pole is slowly tilting toward the east. This distinction between the longitudes of the beginning locations of the sidereal and tropical zodiacs is referred to as Ayanamsha. The beginning points of the tropical and sidereal zodiacs are aligned once about every 25,800 years. According to precise mathematical calculations, the present shift was first observed in 285 AD, i.e. 285 years ago, the North Pole was perfectly vertical at 90 degrees. The most precise method for measuring this ayanamsa Chitrapaksha Ayanamsa. It is also known as Lahiri Ayanamsa.

The ayanamsa calculations made by the Greeks such as Hippocras as well as Ptolemy were not correct. Western scientists are officially recognized as having discovered the precise shifting of Earth's equinox towards the close during the 18th century. They discovered it was 50. This was well-known to Hindu Astrologers long before. Varahamihira was the astrologer of renown at the time of Vikramaditya in the year 57BC, has clearly noted within his book Pancha Siddhantik that was that is based upon our ancient Siddhantas that the ayanamsa time is 50.32 seconds. The most exact one.

The difference between Sayana longitudes as well as those of the Nirayana longitudes that are found in the Planets is known as Ayanamsa also known as precision. This Ayanamsa difference is the exact calculated tilt or shift of the equinox. For instance, on this day on June 23, it is the precise Ayanamsa or angle is 23:58.43°. The longitude poison is caused by the planets of the Zodiac in the present once this Ayanamsa is subtracted from the correct length of the planets appropriate to our position on the earth. The western system is the one that we are in. this shift in the equinox does not take into consideration, all planets are approximately 24-degrees ahead.

There are three different types of styles for charting in India.

In India the astrologers have different ways of casting charts. There are four main methods for casting charts. They will be explained below.

South Indian Style

The south Indian way of casting charts, the location of the zodiacal signs between Aries to Pisces always remains the same as seen in the image to the left. The counting of houses and the placement of the planets are performed clockwise as illustrated in the image below right. This varies from chart to chart. This means South style charts is based on the fixed sign system. The sign that is the ascendant or the lagna is identified by these words: As Or Asc, or Lagna.

North Indian Style

The north Indian way of casting the chart the ascendant or lagna is placed at the top of the chart as well as the significations are identified by their zodiacal number sequence, i.e., Aries is 1. Taurus is 2 Gemini 3. Cancer 4. Leo 5. Virgo 6 Libra 7 Scorpio Sagittarius 9 Capricorn 10. Aquarius 11, and Pisces 12. The charting of the houses and the planets are counter-clockwise. It is possible to affirm that the northern chart is based on the fixed house method.

East Indian or Maithili style

This kind of chart, that is very well-known across Andhra Pradesh and parts of Orissa and Bengal it is drawn in a different manner and is based on the fixed sign technique of the south-style chart, however, the charting is performed counter-clockwise.

## 10. PLANETARY periods (Vimshottari dasha)

Vimshottari Dasa in addition to Manual Calculations

To identify the timing of an of the event, we need to be aware of the time period that is controlled by the significator planet. There are a variety that are dasha system. However, it has been found that Vimshottari dasha is the most reliable. The system is based on length of Moon. Dasa's total duration of 120 years. Ancient sages discovered the lifespan of humans to be around 120 years. Today, it is confirmed by scientists of the present time. They have examined a specific organ, and found that it could function for 120 years. The scientists are also agreed that the longest longevity of a human being can be between 120 and 120 years old. older. The whole time of 120 years is allotted to nine planets. Rahu as well as Ketu are both planets, however they aren't planets.

There are both inner in addition to outer planets. Inner planets refer to planets that lie that lie between the Earth as well as the Sun including those of the Sun, Mercury, Venus and the Moon. Ketu is also part of these inner planets. Mars, Jupiter Saturn are outer planets. Rahu is considered to be an outer planet too. 120 years are divided into two equal pieces with 60-year intervals, and divided between the outer and inner planets. Beginning with Revati that is the ruling planet of Mercury and then Ketu, Venus, Sun and Moon and allotting 17 years, 7 years 20, 20 years, 6 years and 10 years each for 60 years in total? And then Outer Planets, Mars 7 years, Rahu 18 years, Jupiter 16 years, Saturn 19 years for an additional 60 years.

Mercury -----------17 years ago
Ketu----------------7 years
Venus -------------20 years ago
Sun ----------------6 Years
Moon -------------10 year
Mars ---------------7 years ago
Rahu --------------18 years old
Jupiter -----------16 years ago
Saturn ------------19 years ago

Total years 120

The periodsare referred to as the (Main Periods). They are further subdivided into sub-periods. The division of each of the sub period planets is proportional to the period of its birth. One division, however, is one from the Lord. The sub-period can be determined in the following formula:

If M=period, then M = period

Let S be the sub-lord of the period.

Let s = outcome of sub-period in decimal years that can be transformed into days and months.

The formula is now M S x M divided by 120.

For instance, we would like to locate the sub period of Mercury in the Main Period of Saturn. If we take a look at this table, we will see it that Saturn (M) is 19 years, while Mercury (S) is 17 years.

S = M X divided by 120

S = 19 X17 divided by 120

S = 2.6916666

This is equivalent to 2 years, 8 months and 9 days.

However, there's an easier method of doing this: divide the formula in the beginning in 10 and not 12. This will instantly provide you with the months. Let's see.

Months of the year= M S x M multiplied by 10
Number of months = 19 17 X 17 divided by 10

The number of months equals 32.3

The 32.3 is equivalent to that 32 years in total .3 months. 3 x 3, which is 9 consecutive days

Now we can see that 32 months equals the sum of 2 years plus eight months (plus the 9 days) This is exactly the same result in the formula we used before, when we divided by 12.

This is possible orally too, however we must be aware of the time period first.

Let's say, for example, we take Rahu. If we decide to include the sub-period of Rahu within the time of Rahu then we'll have this:

RAHU = 18 Rahu Sub period= 18

Total = 324(leave out the 4)

Take out the number 4 that is 4 so that the remaining is 32. This is the months in a year which is then converted to two years and eight months.

Then, multiply the last digit of number by three. This gives you the days. So, the sub-period for Rahu within the Rahu Mahadasha is 2 years. 8 months 12 days.

Mars subs in Mars Main = 7X7 = 49, which is four years and 27 days.

49/10 equals 4.9which amounts to four months, and 27 (9 3.) days.

Moon subin Moon main = 6 X 10 = 60 = 6 months zero days

In the above equation, one can determine the sub-period of any planet.

Imagine that the main phase of Venus begins at the beginning of January. 1980. It runs up to 20 years. Now , we must find the sub-period in Mars located in Venus main.

Add the years total that comprise Venus and Sun + Moon all the way to Mars equals 20 plus 6+10 = 36 .

Now we must determine the beginning of the Mars subperiod. Therefore, we multiply 36 times 20 (the principal duration of Venus) 36 20 x 720. This leaves the final digit, which provides us with the number 72 (months) equals 6 years. The 720 number is days, which gives the day zero.

That means the Mars subperiod will begin 6 years following the 1st of January 1980, which will be the 1st of January 1986.And this means the Mars time frame will comprise 7 20 x 20 = 140 = one year and two months.

In the same way, we can locate the sub-period of any planet within either the primary as well as the Mahadasha timeframe of every planet.

It is believed that the Vimshottari Mahadasha is founded on the area of the Moon that it is located and utilizes the angular distance of every Nakshatra that is 13 degrees. 20 min.

Conversion Table

Aries---------------0 deg
Taurus------------30deg
Gemini-----------60deg
Cancer------------90deg
Leo---------------120deg
Virgo-------------150deg
Libra--------------180deg
Scorpio-----------210deg
Sagittarius--------240deg
Capricorn---------270deg
Aquarius----------300deg
Pisces--------------330deg

Analyzing the results of SUB-PERIOD LORDS

The events are accelerated during sub-periods for significant planets. It is therefore crucial to understand how to analyze the diea (main period) and the bhukti (sub-period) outcomes. The outcomes of the general significance of the lord of sub-periods depend on its strength, position in conjunction with the same. The house of the placement is affected when transit planets bring beneficial or negative effects on the sub-period Lord. When a planet is in the sub-period planet, they have the following significance.

(1) The main meaning for the sun is its general meaning. For instance, the Sun determines the father's social status, status with the

government, male children digestion system and heart, blood pressure and more.

(2) The significance of the home where the mooltrikona signification of the planet in question is located. If that in the house of the mooltrikona sign the planet of a malefic is located or a malefic planet is in the vicinity of the most effective area of the house and the house is in period of the sub-periods afflicting or afflicted planets, the meaning of the house with the sign mooltrikona is not going to be prosperous and will be faced with problems attributed to the planet that is affected by the Lordship.

(3) The meaning of the house in which the planet is situated.

(4) When a planet is in the sub-period of a planet, all effects on the house, that is home to the MT sign for the planet, are also brought into effect. Due to the effects on MEP by a powerful functional benefic planet, even the sub-period of a weak planet could favor the native with excellent or extremely good results. A similar contact of a functional malefic Planet on MEP(most impacting point) of the MT sign house might cause the planet ruling the MT(mooltrikona) signhouse to have positive results in its sub-periods, even if the planet ruling it is strong in the chart of birth.

## 11. TRANSIT (Gochar) of planets and their impact on our lives

Transit is among the most important tools used to predict of the future of events. They can also be useful in timing events as that are not indicated by other methods, like the ones that are indicated by a direction or progression.

Transits are the movement of a luminary, planet or any other astrological element across another point or planet which is typically derived is derived from a birth chart. It indicates how changes in the present which are symbolized by the object or the planet, are related to the individualas depicted in the chart of birth as a whole and the specific natal planet or point. The transiting planet or point creates some kind of angle ("aspect") with the birth planet or point. The angle in question provides clues as to how the relationship.

### MAKE PREDICTIONS IN ASTROLOGY Utilizing TRANSITS

Within Vedic Astrology one of the most reliable methods is the one known as Transit. The fundamental method of using this method is simple to first identify the zodiacal positions of planets on any date that is that is being considered, and then use these planetary positions and then compare them with the locations of the planets in the way when they existed at date when the person was born (i.e. your birth chart). The resultant pattern is then analyzed for any effects that result from the interactions of the transiting planets and the birth chart.

The most important aspect of this method of prediction is knowing what will happen when a specific planet interacts with the pre-existing pattern of planetary movement on the birth chart. The first step is to look at the house (area of existence) the planet transiting through will affect by changing its zodiacal sign in the chart of birth.

Let's look at an example If Jupiter is in Capricorn throughout 2009 (using the sidereal zodiac) as well as the chart of birth of your child is Leo Rising, which makes Capricorn the sign of the 6th house The transit of Jupiter is which is the planet that brings prosperity as well as growth can be expected to increase opportunities in the field of employment for this person.

Beyond the basic effects that are triggered by the sign or house in which the planet is transiting in, we can look at how the planet in transit interacts with other parts of the zodiac, and in turn, the chart of birth. In the present example that follows: Jupiter is believed in Vedic Astrology to have a significant affect (aspect) all signs (and consequently the houses) which are situated in both the fifth and ninth positions relative to the planet itself (called"trines", i.e. around 120 degrees from it) Then each of Virgo and Taurus benefit from Jupiter's transit within Capricorn. According to Leo's Leo rising chart both signs are the 2nd and 10th houses. i.e. the Income (the second) along with the Career (the 10th). Therefore, at this stage in the analysis we find that those who are born under Leo rising signs are more likely to make more money when they work due to jobs in 2009.

The following part of the analysis will determine whether the planet that is transiting is in contact in any way with the chart of birth' natal planets. Each planet has its own natural meaning. For example, Venus is the planet of Love and Romance. By using the example of Jupiter moving through Capricorn If your birth chart contains Venus in Capricorn 2009 is expected to provide opportunities (Jupiter) to Love and Romance (Venus). If we continue to look towards our Leo ascending chart then the romantic aspect will be evident within the sixth house of work, i.e., a relationship with an employee or a colleague.

Another illustration: Mars is one of the planets that move at a speed faster than others that takes about six weeks to traverse the zodiac's sign. When we transpose the sign in which Mars is currently transiting through the Heavens to the chart of birth that we are looking at, we can figure the part of the chart that the individual Mars will impact during its stay in the zodiac sign. Because Mars represents the Planet of Energy and Action, its transit is usually accompanied by tangible results that are important to keep on top of. As of the time of posting, Mars is transiting in Sagittarius. In any place that Sagittarius appears within the Vedic Astrology birth chart, that area of your life will be charged. If you're Sagittarius rising in the zodiac, then the word you should be looking for is Action during all six weeks that follow Mars passing across your sign of ascendance. Mars enjoys physical activities which is why keeping yourself busy is vital. Mars is also a combative animal Beware of an urge to fight with others. Mars as a character in Vedic Astrology is thought to be able to project all of its force towards itself, so the movement that occurs of Mars in Sagittarius influences Pisces too. Because Pisces constitutes the 4th House in the Sagittarius rising chart of the person, Mars transit puts stress on the activities that involve the home and also creates the possibility of conflicts with mother.

As compared to celestial bodies Moon can move very quickly and takes more than 2 days for it to traverse the sign. The Vedic system of Astrology it is believed that the Moon is considered to be of paramount significance in determining the events that occur on Earth. This is why it is no surprise that the Moon is given a special place when it comes to studying transits. Its influence is most evident when it is in the sign that is already occupied the planet that is transiting, and typically, it is responsible for activating the event that was promised through analysis of other planets' positions. This is why the Moon is the second hand on the universe's clock. In the case of the year to come the year 2009 Jupiter is expected to be through Capricorn. The Moon will be in Capricorn for about two consecutive days each lunar cycle i.e. roughly every month. Whatever Jupiter is indicating by its passage within a specific area of a chart for natal birth this potential is greatly enhanced as the Moon is in Capricorn every month. If we keep an eye on the Moons place of transit, we are able to identify the most likely dates for the events that are connected to the particular event we want to forecast for.

If multiple transits occur in the same sign, or that affect a sign via aspect, the energy available for events rises; especially if there is an interaction between the natal planets of someone's birth chart. Even though the chance of something happening is high but predicting precisely what is going to occur becomes more difficult as there are many different meanings of the planets in interaction with one and each other. This is the place where the Vedic Astrologer has to use the various methods and formulas that are used to evaluate the quality and power of each planet transiting in a particular constellation in order to determine which planet have the upper hand and thus will dominate the result. Being able to accurately predict the interactions of planets with one another is the principal topic of both old and contemporary texts about astrology. It is also is an area that requires constant investigation and research by all Astrologers.

In particular, the current phase of Saturn in Leo will be undergoing a time that is more likely to trigger negative events as a result of the planet being in its retrograde phase during the beginning of the first six months of the year. Because Saturn is simultaneously ruled to the Heavens by the Uranus transit in Aquarius in early 2009 The dates on which the Moon is transiting between Leo or Aquarius result in a higher chance of major events occurring within the world. If, within a person's natal chart is there any planets within the last levels in Leo or Aquarius or Aquarius, the person is likely to be susceptible to an unpleasant incident to happen in their life, specifically on days that the Moons transit is a source of additional activation. The affected house will indicate which area of life the incident is expected to take place within.

Twelve celestial bodies to consider (if we take into account three outer planets Uranus, Neptune, and Pluto along with Rahu as well as Ketu) It is evidently a challenge to determine what is going to take place on any particular day. It becomes even more difficult when the positions of transits are compared to the image of the chart of birth. Astrologers then focus on the particular transit that is dominating the current situation. It is important to note that the pattern of the birth chart is a permanent feature to it. In a sense it is an element of resistance to the impacts of the planets that are transiting. However, if a strong planet, like Saturn or Mars or Jupiter, comes into close proximity to a particular planet or sensitive points, or activated house on a birth chart, then it is important to be aware. The transit is a dynamic pattern within the Heavens like the work of the Celestial Clock; it is through studying the astrological system that we are able to keep track of time.

## Chapter 5: Retrograde (Vakra) Planets

Apart from other than the Sun as well as the Moon the other stars, Mars, Mercury, Jupiter, Venus and Saturn alter their normal motions through the Zodiac often and appear to reverse. After a while, they return to their normal motion. When a planet goes retrograde, it is identified in the horoscope by the letter "R". Retrograde planets are more strong. It also produces some odd outcomes, sometimes in reverse order of the timing of effects, etc.

The effect of retrograde planets in Horoscope

If a person's birth occurs during a time when the planet is moving in retrograde the person is greatly dependent on the planet's attributes. If more than one planet is has been retrograde during the birth then the planet that has the highest amount of degrees within its signs will affect the individual more.

1. If an object is retrograde within its most exalted position, the planet loses power to assist the native.

2. If an object is retrograde in its debilitating sign, it gains more strength and assists its natives in all ways

3. When a planet appears to be debilitated or retrograde Navamsa chart, but elsewhere in the Rashi chart, it will help

4. Natural benefics (Jupiter,Venus,Mercury,Moon) if own 4,7,10 houses from Ascendant and are retrograde, then will cause more problems in all aspects to the houses they own and also the house they're placed in.

5. Nature malefics (Sun,Mars,Saturn) If you have houses with 4,7,10 from Ascendant as well as retrograde then they'll bring have positive results in all areas of the homes they reside in as well as the home they're in.

6. A planet that has 1,5,9 houses(they shouldn't have 6,8,12 houses simultaneously) in retrograde, will be beneficial to the individual.

7. The planets (except Jupiter) give results of the home they began in retrograde, however not of the place they were placed in when they were born. Only Jupiter provides

The results of the same house in which it was built at birth.

### 13. COMBUST (Asta) planets

Planets that lose some their strength due to their being in close proximity to Sun are known as Combust planets in Vedic Astrology or "Aast" Grahas as in vedic astrology (Jyotish). Planets that are not combust but not considered to be 'Aast' and are referred to as 'Udit'.

Effect of Combust planets in horoscopes

Brihat Parasara Hora Shastra explains," If ascendant lord is suffering from debilitation, burning or in enemy sign there are diseases. (Sloka 2 and 3 "Effects upon Tanu Bhava).This verse focuses on the significance of combustion in the natal horoscopy. There are two distinct moudhyas that give importance for Venus in addition to Jupiter. When Jupiter is in combust Upanayana (reborn-ceremony) cannot be performed. The other planets, however, don't enjoy the same respect in the same way. when Mercury is in the process of combusting, you must have informed your panchanga that certain days are not ideal for schooling, journalism and court proceedings. If Saturn is combust it ought to have warned that you should not sign an employment contract.

A combustion Venus is thought to create losses in the business. That means that if you decide to purchase a pair of shoes, you'll be faced with losses; the storekeeper is also liable for losses. Losses and losses all over. Because Mercury and Venus are close to the Sun this phenomenon occurs often, if not every year. In this situation, it's a good idea to look at the trade activities at that point. The period of burning by the Panchanga has not resulted in slowing trade, divorces and divorces. There is a chance that you won't lose anything, nor will the profits of the shopkeepers - since the shops may close due to a variety of reasons, either national or natural. A situation like this, taken from a national fiscal perspective, isn't bad at all, but when the flames are burning there is a chance that we have to traverse such a period.

"If the planets lose their strength as a result of combustion, the person who is affected will be admitted to into the Holy Order, which means he will be saintly" (sloka five "Ascetism Yogas" Brihat Parasara Hora Shastra). It's not all negative about combustion. For instance, if you have a powerful Venus in your chart, the impact of combustion is not as severe. When a planet is burned, it loses its power to the Sun.In the case where Sun has a positive aspect such as 5th lord or 9th lord 10th or 11th lord and so on. What happens when the effects of this combustion influence you? The good news will be spread from the significance associated with Venus and the issues that are represented by the Sun will prosper. However, the inherent significance (beauty aesthetics, beauty and elegance that the indigenous) will be harmed by the combustion. Other aspects should be taken into account." If 11thLord is elevated, even in the event of a fire, there are many benefits". (sloka 2 "Effects from Labha Bhava" Brihat Parasara Shastra).

## 14. The IMPACT of Rahu and Ketu's the birth chart

### The RAHU (Moon's North Node)

Rahu as well as Ketu are two planets that are considered to be shadowy. The two places where the Moon's orbit Moon passes through the ecliptic are named Rahu or Ketu. Ecliptic is the apparent route of the Sun when seen from Earth. Rahu is known as the as the ascending node of Moon in the Western Astrology. Ketu is referred to as the descender in the Moon in western Astrology.

The impact on Rahu or Ketu on the chart of birth is extremely important for the individual. Rahu along with Ketu are usually unfavourable planets. They pose challenges in their sub-periods or extended transit influences. They expose the person to over-ambition, anxiety and sudden setbacks. They can also lead to inadvertent health problems food poisoning, loss of fame allergies, loss due to cheating and inflammation, setbacks in professional careers and depression, strains in business relationships, persistent diseases, losses as a result of speculation or risky ventures are prone to sexually transmitted infections and black magic issues and evil spirits, litigation, unexpected accidents and difficulties in your marriage.

Positive Results During Rahu's Sub-Periods

Rahu produces good results only if it is situated in the right houses i.e. apart from the dusthana house (sixth, eighth and twelfth house) It is not in conjunction with any planet, the midpoint of the house or to any other planet, and its swaying is powerful. Rahu is a person who is determined and encourages him/her to make more effort to reach the goals he/she has set. The effect of Rahu on a planet can enhance the effects of the planet.

Degree that is rising in ascendency is taken to be the level that indicates the most efficient point of every house. Rahu's placement within 5 degrees of the ascending point in each of the houses is considered to be in close proximity with the most efficient point, and is affects the houses of placement as well as aspects. If it is placed correctly, Rahu in a good house and without causing any affliction and with a strong disposition has good results in the pursuit of material things within the sub-periods. Sometimes, however the positive effects of materialistic Rahu disappear after the initial gains. If Rahu is Rahu is in ascendant position, it stimulates the individual, making him enthusiastic and eager for increasing his earnings without concern for the ethical codes of the society that he lives in. If you are in the house of second it transforms the native into politician who is trying to achieve the status in whatever area he finds himself in.In the house of the Third it enhances courage and initiative and also indicates prosperity in material terms for younger brothers.

When it comes to the 4th house it makes one want to acquire new vehicles, assets and to use even unjust methods to advance educational and profession matters.In the 5th house it is a sign of the benefits of speculation and excellent intuition faculty.In the 7th house it signifies the celebration of marriage joy in the marriage relationship, and relationships that are not based on the marriage bond, and traveling to abroad places.In the 9th house it is a sign of participation in religious events and the desire for moksha , but without the necessary sincere efforts.In the tenth, it makes one a diplomat and a skilled public relations person, and an ambitious person who can achieve his goals through the use and use of vices.In the eleventh place it provides unearned profits through manipulative and corrupted tendencies.

The close connection and aspect Rahu to a beneficent functionally solid, well-placed planet strongly activates the meaning of the planet concerned and can result in extremely short-lived and dramatic results.

Affliction of Planets

When Rahu creates close conjunction/aspect with natal planets it triggers affliction and takes away the significance the planets. The damage is less if the planets that are afflicted are strong, but more so than when they're weak. If these planets have weak positions, poorly placed , and closely afflicted by Rahu this is a sign of tragic events. If the conjunction/aspect is within a difference in longitudinal that is one degree wide, issues occur in the first sub-period Rahu as well as the other planet that is afflicted by Rahu. If this affliction occurs within five degrees to one side or the other, this result can be felt at a very young time in the sub-period of the planet affected or Rahu.

If the conjunction is large it can only be felt at the end of life. If Rahu is afflicted by the Sun this can indicate problems with father, son husband, husband, blood pressure, and the character. Rahu's relationship with Venus suggests problems with spouse, marital relationships as well as partnerships, kidneys, as well as educational pursuits.Rahu's condition of the Moon indicates an unwell and troubled mind as well as heart problems as well as problems for spouse and mother as well as disagreements over property. It is necessary to travel to distant places and be afflicted by home-sickness. Rahu's illness of Mars results in wealth, arouses the dynamism and courage of a person as well as diseases of impurity of blood, and troubles for younger brothers. Rahu's illness of Mercury can cause skin diseases and nerve problems, as well as paralysis, lunacy, digestive problems, constipation, and confusion. Rahu's condition of Jupiter causes problems with the liver and pancreas, which reduces hearing capacity as well as makes people self-centered and morally unsound, creates issues to husbands, sons as well as fathers and creates an unpopular image. Rahu's illness of Saturn is a sign of labor issues with bad reputation, rheumatism asthma, excessive cough and breathing issues. Physical problems are more severe when the lord of the ascendant's position is weak and poorly located and infected.

Results of Rahu not causing any harm in Dusthanas

Rahu is placed within the house of sixth during the sub-period is a sign of undiagnosed ailments and intestinal issues, loss from fire and theft issues in the profession or job and incompatible relationships with family members. If it is placed in the 8th house, in its sub-periods it can cause deaths in the family, financial losses family disintegration, and impedes the ability to live a healthy life. Rahu in the 12th house is a risk for gamble addiction, and gives the threat of prison, loss and expenses, problems with hypertension, and a tense family peace at the most efficient place. This can cause health issues as well as losses from gambling, a tendency to over consumption of material goods mental turmoil and a problem to parents.

The results of Rahu or Ketu when they are afflicting Dusthanas

Rahu or Ketu in the event of being placed close to the most powerful spot of one of the malefic houses , or creating severe illness for some other planet, its consequences can be extremely severe. In their sub-periods, in addition to having a negative effect on the symbol of the planet that is affected the planet, they can also be a sign of undiagnosed or long-term health issues, intestinal issues, loss due to fire or theft, issues with work or profession, unbalanced relationships with family members from other families and death within the family or disintegration of families issues for parents, and impedes the living space, and makes one susceptible to addiction and gambling and the threat of prison costs and losses, the problems with hypertension, deeply troubled domestic peace, loss by cheating, the tendency to an excessive amount of indulgence in materialism infringements, antisocial and law-breaking actions or mental disorders and difficulties with the law.

Afflicting RAHU throughout the houses

If Rahu is afflicted by the mid-point in a house with a mooltrikona sign as well as the disposer weak, it will cause damage is felt in all the houses listed below.

First House:

Physical degeneration and acute health issues, problems in marriage, and issues for fathers and male children.

Second House:

Family disintegration divorce loss of status fame and wealth digestive issues and difficulties to fathers.

Third House:

Illegal acts, slander and slandering, marital problems slow physical growth issues for fathers and earning by illegal methods.

Fourth House:

Disrupts peace at home and prevents professional development, causing unfortunate events and accidents as well as wasteful expenditures and losses.

Fifth House:

The loss of semen, the absence or progeny and issues to the father or elder brother, and self. Earnings from unsuitable methods.

Sixth House:

Chronic disease, stomach ulcer acidity, loss due to fires and thefts, threats of prison, conflicts and disruption in family life.

Seventh House:

Extra marital relations, poor health of spouse and self venereal and skin conditions, issues to brothers, and the use of illegal gambling and other practices.

Eighth House:

Involvement in scandals, accidents and family conflicts, separation eyes, piles and loss of peace in the home.

Ninth House:

Troubles with self parents, fathers, children and their younger brothers. It is a complete moral blunder. People resort to vices and gambling.

Tenth House:

Causes termination as a result of corruption and destroys assets, causes problems with blood pressure and renders the person in charge an untruthful person.

Eleventh House:

The exploitation of money through corruption can affect the spouses' health and causes problems in marriage relations. Native employs unfair methods and conducts business in a misleading manner.

Twelfth House:

It makes one an addict and gambler. The threat of jail loss and expense The problem of hypertension deeply disturbed domestic peace.

Impact of Transit on Rahu

The influence of transit on Rahu is in some ways suggestive of tensions and conflicts. Transit relationships through close conjunction and conjunction to weak planets can be evident when the longitudinal distance is five degrees and is in the situation that is grave at the precise conjunction or aspect.

The tension/trouble begins as the relationship develops and is ended when it breaks away from the aspect or close conjunction. When there is a good and well-positioned natal and transit planets, the distance of the aspect or conjunction is just one degree. The impact is felt according to the following factors:

1. The significance of the homes where mooltrikona signs from troubled planets are situated.

2. The universal symbolism of the planet inflicted.

3. The universal meaning of the house in which the affected planet is situated.

4. The most common meaning of houses of conjunction as well as the houses that are aspected, if the conjunction is situated at the strongest aspect of the house.

The effect is more severe the more Rahu the transiting planet is in dusthanas, and when the planets/houses concerned are weak in both natal as well as transit charts.

Rahu's close association with Venus is a trigger to indulge in sexual pleasures during the first phases of life. It also encourages enjoyment with alcohol and smoking or intoxication via other methods or other means. Rahu's involvement in the most potent points of the seventh, third fifth, and eighth houses leads the person to carnal pleasures prior to marriage and romantic relationships only for the pleasure of physical pleasure. Rahu's close relationship with Mercury along with the deficient Moon within the 8th or twelfth house is what makes one a addict. I am sure that readers will gain from this, in defining the positions of Rahu in particular birth.

SPECULATION as well as RAHU

Gains are governed through the house of the eleventh. The gains from investments are controlled through the 5th house.

There are no other houses. Also, If there isn't a mooltrikona sign , then the houses are examined to determine the other influences that have influenced the houses, such as occupation and other factors.

The sphere of speculation is controlled by Rahu. Its intensity could be rising due to the increasing influence of Rahu in a specific chart. The effect of Mercury could involve people who are involved in the speculation of shares and stocks. The impact of Mars could involve the person engaged in speculation about properties.

Rahu rules greed, speculation, gambling,impersonification, misrepresentation, selfishness, cheating, manufacturing of spurious articles, copying and manipulations. The benefits gained by using the methods mentioned are not long time and eventually lead to losses which cause a lot of pain to the individual.

Influence of Rahu creates risk orientation or gambling tendencies. Sometimes, it's calculated risk. Other times, it's blind risk. The effect of poorly placed planets creates blind risk.

The Houses 1st, 3rd 5th, and 10th are linked to the actions of a person. Therefore, the influence of these the planets that rule the actions provides the tendency to take risks in life. Positively, the effect is entrepreneurial and growth-oriented.

The powerful influence of Rahu is a wide-ranging influence because of close conjunction or aspect. It may be present throughout the third fourth, fifth 11th, and tenth houses in addition to the ascendant.

If the fourth and fifth houses are strong, or the second, third, fifth and tenth houses appear powerful, then the benefits derived by the individual may be more enduring but ultimately, they're lost.

KETU (moon's South Node)

Ketu is one of the non-luminaries planet in the Vedic Astrology; Ketu is called an chhaya graha (shadowy planet) It doesn't emit any light, and it doesn't reflect light. What is the reason why Vedic Astrology contain non-luminaries? Take a look at the issue of eclipses: When the Moon blocks the Sun The Sun also makes Earth are eclipsed by the Moon. What is the astrological reason behind these events? The moment when lunar orbits cross line of the ecliptic (the celestial equator) At these times the moon's shadows are visible and have an significance for astrology. Lunar Nodes Lunar Nodes show the times when lunar and solar forces oppose each other , or block each other. They also illustrate the need to short-circuit lunar and solar energies.

The effect of KETU on different homes

First House- Thick form with a weak structure, lots of sweat, insecure, slim piles sexual indulgence, sly.

Second house- Bad utterer, quiet, quick in awareness, irritable, hard-hearted, economical.

Third house- daring resilient, durable, and creative wealthy, popular, and affluent.

Fourth house - Argumentative, insecure, and afraid of poisons.

Fifth house- Generous loss of children or children, corrupt, dishonest, if stressed.

Sixth house- Loves the lack of faith, a good communicator neglected, with venereal complaints educated.

Seventh house - Fervent corrupt, insecure connections to widows, sickening wives.

Eighth house: Ridiculous boring, unclear with piles of trouble and similar issues.

Ninth House- Short-sighted and wicked. good-hearted, many children, a good wife.

Tenth house-Fertile mind, happy spiritual, religious, seeker of pilgrimage for sacred places and rivers loved by scriptures.

Eleventh house- Funny, amusing, shameless, brainy, rich.

Twelfth house - Unpredictable, nervous mind, foreign home Attracted to sycophantic lectures and a lot of traveling. It is also spiritual, immoral.

## Chapter 6: Aspects (Drishti) On Planets And Their Impact On The Planets.

When the planets rose over the horizon and look towards each other from the downwards, they exchanged glances. They would face each the other. The planets showed their fullness when they were facing one another, and looking straight at each one. Aspects link or connect the planets.

Vedic Astrology uses a complete signification, which means that the sign is an house. The planets are a part of the houses, either with or without planets. All planets are in alignment with the house or the planets in opposing positions (7th). Planets that are in the same sign or house meet (conjunction).

The planets encircle the entire sign. The influence is greater with orbs nearer. Planets that are not in their sign but in the same degrees still affect each one another. Vedic Astrology uses specific features for the planets Mars, Saturn, and Jupiter . Mars has a direct connection to the 4th and 8th house away from its own. Saturn is in the 3rd and the 10th house. Jupiter has a direct connection with the 5th and 9th houses. They are all considered to be full aspects. Full aspects are regarded as 100 percent influential. There are weaker aspects of 75-50 percent, which are seldom used. Every aspect is cast a forward direction. Rahu as well as Ketu (not known by any Vedic Astrologers) similar to Jupiter are trines that rule the 5th as well as 9th house. The aspects themselves have the significance associated with the planets. They are not a source of meaning. They are the connectors of the energy of the planet. Thus, Rahu and Ketu transmit the negative energy to the house or planet they align, but which is not the purpose of a trine, as per Western Astrology.

The significance of each planet differs from chart to chart. The variance for each of the planets is determined through:

1.) Does it have a natural benefit or a malign one?

2.) Does it function as a positive or negative?

This is based on houses that they govern in the chart. Mars is a possible beneficial for Cancer ascendant since it governs the auspicious 5th House (trikona) and it is the home of the 10th. Jupiter is a potential negative for Taurus ascendant due to its rule over the challenging 8th house along with the 11th. The planets represent the meanings for the homes they govern. They cast their influences to the houses and planets that reside therein, they imbibe these houses/planets with all the energy they have. If the planet is in opposition to another this can alter the planet's meaning.

When planets align with an area, it will rule. This gives it an additional force to the benefit of that house. It's like the planet being within the same house, but in its own way.

The planets may mutually affect each with respect to each other. This is often the case with conjunction and opposition as well as with particular aspects

For example: Mars in Capricorn, and Saturn in Aries. In this case, Mars faces Saturn via its 4th aspect, while Saturn influences Mars through its 10th aspect. They both aspect one another. This is a two-way relationship.

If planets are in their respective ruler's ship, referred to as reciprocal reception also known as Parivartana This is an extremely powerful connection. In addition, if the planets additionally aspected, it is even more potent. The complete connection is known as Sambandha.

The above example is a case of Mars situated in Capricorn as well as Saturn within Aries is found in Sambandha. They are in mutual aspect and are both in the same signs (mutual perception). Another instance would be The Sun in Aquarius and Saturn in Leo. They both face each other by opposing forces, and are also in each other's sign.

If Mars is located in the 4th house, it faces to the opposing house which is the 10th. Mars is a special aspect. It's the 8th and 4th houses that are separated from it. Mars on the 4th aspect the 7th and 11th. Then put Saturn within the 5th House. From there, it will aspect the opposite house, the 11th. In particular, Saturn will be in the 3rd and 10th houses from its own. Saturn is in the 7th and 2nd house. In this instance, the 7th and 11th house will be influenced from all three planets. These two houses are bursting with activity even though there aren't any planets in them. The results is likely to be mixed because of the various planetary energies. Thus, the natural beneficial qualities as well as the temporal characteristics of these planets will impact these houses.

Temporal characteristics are based on the houses in which the planets govern. In this case, the 7th and 11th houses are ruled by the aspect of the natural positive Jupiter and the naturally positive Mars as well as Saturn. When the ascension is Gemini, Jupiter rules two Kendras (angles 7 and 10, and). Saturn is the ruler of on the 8th as well as the 9th. The rulers of the 5th, 1st and the 9th always are positive influence on the chart. Because Saturn is the 8th ruler, it could cause problems with the 8th house. Saturn is considered to be a functional benefic in this. Mars is considered to be a malefic planet for Gemini ascendant, as it rules the 6th and 11th. However, in this instance Mars is the ruler of the 11th, and is in conjunction with the 11th. It's going to act as if that it's in its sign, in the 11th. Mars is expected to energize the 11th house in the way it can bring (great gains and friendships). In this case, Jupiter is in the 7th house, and controls seven houses. This is good for the 7th house issues (marriage).

Once all the aspects have been reviewed in the Rashi chart, they need to be examined using the Moon to further clarify the situation.

The planets that transit as they are facets to the birth planets trigger the happenings in the course of a life.

The aspects act as connectors for energy of the planets. The planets contain every house they govern and also the aspects they receive.

20. YOGKARAKA planet in birth chart

In accordance with the principles of Vedic astrology, also known as Jyotish according to the rules of Jyotish or Vedic astrology, the Yogakaraka is the planet that is the ruler of the Kendra house as well as Trikona house. The known as Kendra houses are the houses with angular angles in western Astrology, i.e., the 1st 4, 4th, 7th and 10th. These are considered as the four most important houses of the chart because they symbolize that the "Cross of the Matter" where the soul is entombed in this present existence. Every day, there is a Sun is rising (1st house). Then it culminates (10th house). Culminates (10th house). Sets (7th house) and anti-culminates (4th house). These so-called Trikona houses comprise two of them that create the trine (120 degree) connection to the ascendant. These are the 5th in addition to the 9th. These Trikona houses are thought to be among the most fortunate areas and are the source of all wisdom, talent as well as guidance, inspiration and creativity.

With the above description, it is clear that any planet which has the rulership of both the house of Kendra and the Trikona house is likely to be a significant and positive influence on the life of the person who is affected. It could be a for success and growth in the world and its position in relation to sign, house, and other aspects shouldn't be neglected.

YOGKARAKA PLANETS for a variety of different ages

It is not possible for every planet to be considered yogakaraka, as not every rising sign can provide the right conditions for it. Here are the most relevant rising signs as well as the yogakaraka planets:

Based on the above chart the yogakaraka planet has lordship over two houses: the Kendra and the Trikona house in half of rising signs, whereas in the remaining fifty percent of all signs, there isn't a single planet that is able to be an yogakaraka. The planets Sun, Mercury and Jupiter are not able to turn into yogakaraka. For Rahu and Ketu when they are part of a Kendra or receiving an aspect from, or are associated with the Lord of the Trikona or Kendra or Trikona, they can attain yogakaraka status.

21. The DISPOSITOR of any planet within the birth chart

The Ruler of the Sign at the edge of a House is the one who disposes of, or is the disposer of a planet that is posited within that House. If the person who is dispositor of a planet that is considered to be an indication, is removed through the ruler of Ascendant it is considered to be a positive signification. In the case of a Solar panel it is said that the ruler of the sign represents the dispositor for the planet that is posited in it. It is believed that whenever a star is placed in the Sign which is ruled by an other planet, the latter is believed to be influenced by the planet ruling the Sign within which it is situated, the result, it alters its character. Therefore in the event that Saturn happens to be in the Sign that is ruled by Jupiter and Jupiter's Jupiter ascendant influence can be believed to be permeating the Saturn influence, making its influence more Jupiter ascendants, and lesser Saturn ascendants. The idea is stated as if "Saturn is destroyed to Jupiter," or that "Jupiter is the savior of Saturn." The definitions given by various sources are unclear and appear to be contradictory, however an examination of the older texts seems to justify the straightforward explanation that is provided here. Of course, the word must not be taken too literally, as the majority of experts believe that a planet that is actually an House is more powerful in its influence on the actions of the House than the Ruler of the Sign at its cusp, or an incoming Sign within the House. The degree to that the Dispositor blocks its influence on the planet it's disposal, is a matter to be judged on the power of aspects as well as the nature of the planets in the aspect in relation to the Dispositor as well as the planet that it is disposed.

Disposal for different ascendants
Sun is in Sagittarius (ruled by Jupiter)
Moon located in Scorpio (ruled by Pluto)

Mercury is in Capricorn (ruled by Saturn)
Venus is located in Scorpio (ruled by Pluto)
Mars is located in Leo (ruled by the Sun)
Jupiter is located in Cancer (ruled by the Moon)
Saturn is in Capricorn (ruled by Saturn)
Uranus is located in Aries (ruled by Mars)
Neptune is in Virgo (ruled by Mercury)
Pluto is located in Cancer (ruled by the Moon)
Or , as we can say
Sun is destroyed by Jupiter
Moon is disposed of by Pluto
Mercury is disposed of by Saturn
Venus is disposed of by Pluto
Mars is destroyed by Sun
Jupiter is deposed by Moon
Saturn is dispossessed by Saturn
Uranus is destroyed by Mars
Neptune is disposed of by Mercury
Pluto is disposed of by Moon

22. The STRENGTH of houses and planets in a specific birth chart (Shadbala)
PLANETS' STRENGTHS
The planets are stronger when they are located in the mid-degree region within the house. This is known as the midpoint.
Naturally , as a planet becomes weak in debilitation, the planet gets stronger in its primary home or the moolatrikona signs. The

strength increases when it is in its elevated state, which is located in the opposite direction of the place where the planet is weak seven houses to the west.

A benefic planet can provide additional power to another planet that are malefic or benefic in a person's natal chart as well as when the planet is in conjunction with or passes over the planet of birth. The benefic planet can only give positive energy that strengthens the planet even if it's weak in any way and also brings lesser negative energy and malefic to a planet that is naturally malefic. The benefic planet can produce similar results when it is in or faces the Dusthana house (six or eight, or 12) and is located close to its midpoint in the ascendant. The benefic planet can decrease its strength when it surrounds it around malefic planets, or in the malefic house, but it is still able to bring benefic energy to malefic planets or houses , thus decreasing the negative impact. It is counter-productive.

The despositor ships determines if the planet that is benefic can achieve its full potential, and when a planet is benefic that is in a moolatrikona sign that isn't weak, there will get good outcomes. For instance, if the planet Jupiter is situated at the Fifth House of the constellation of Libra while the depositor Venus is elevated in the sign of Pisces and Pisces, it is likely that Jupiter can reach the fullest potential.

The planets that are exalted are able to produce amazing results if that the planets aren't vulnerable in any other category, such as navamsa chart, malefic houses, etc. The state of exaltation for a planet could be described as the summer resort. The planet's moolatrikona rays could be considered to be one's primary residence and is enjoyed and used to live comfortably however, in summer time, one is taking a vacation and feels excited and delighted by the thought of staying at his summer home in the countryside, or on the beach. This simple analogy describes the exalted status of a planet which can yield incredible outcomes.

PLANETS' STRENGTHS IN ORDER:

1. If the planets aren't in the early stages of development, they are either at 0-5 degrees or between 25 and 30 degrees..

2. If planets are situated in the range of 10 to 20 degrees within the same sign, they can be very powerful.

3. When planets are in their moolatrikona sign , or primary house.

4. In the case of planets that are under the influence or under the influence of benefic and functional planets.
5. If planets are populated with deposits that are strong.
6. If planets have positive positions in the navamsa or the other charts of division.
7. When planets orbit exaltation signs, which are considered to be the most favorable sign.
8. When planets are not located in negative houses, such as the sixth or twelveth house.

Signification

Planetary strength is essential to chart predictions. Strong planets will show auspicious impacts during their period of influence (Dasas transits). Planets that are weak will have negative impacts.

The strength of Rashi resp. Bhava Lords is a different part of chart. Bhavas can have effects based on their strength as well as the ability of their lords.

Some sources of strength provide tips for specific uses: e.g. Digbala offers information on directions with positive or negative consequences.

Calculation

The total Shadbala is the total from all Balas. They are considered in Rupas and Virupas. One

Rupa includes 60 Virupas. The majority of sources of strength have values ranging from zero the Virupas (very fragile) and a maximum that is 60 Virupas (very robust). Others (like Drekkana Bala) have the maximum value that is 30 Virupas.

Parasara offers the necessary values for strength for every planet. Planets that meet these requirements are considered strong. They will be blessed with favorable results. Planets with weak energy will be not to be favourable.

Shadbala is a variety of Shadbala

There are six main kinds of Shadbala. Sthana Bala and Kala Bala are sub-balas with a variety of sub-balas. The structure (including the translation to Sanskrit terminology) is as follows. Follow the hyperlinks.

1. Sthana Bala - positional strength

1.1 Uchcha Bala - divisional strength

1.2 Saptavargaja Bala - strength of exaltation

1.3 Ojhajugmariamsa Bala strength related to its placement in odd/even Rashis and Navamsas

1.4 Kendradi Balastrength of placement in cadent houses, in angle houses, succedent or cadent houses

1.5 Drekkana Bala - strength in accordance with Drekkana the position of the planets

2. Dig Bala is directional power

3. Kala Bala - - temporal strength

3.1 Nathonatha Bala - diurnal/nocturnal power
3.2 Paksha Bala - strength that is related to the lunar phase
3.3 Tribhaga Bala - strength associated with parts of the night/day
3.4 Varsha-Masa-Dina-Hora Bala - strength of astrological year month day and hour
3.5 Yudhdha Bala power resulting from global conflict
3.6 Ayana Bala - equinoctial strength
4. Cheshta Bala is a motional force
5. Naisargika Bala - natural strength
6. Drig Bala - strength of the aspect

## Chapter 7: Diffrent Yoga In Birth Chart

Astrologically, yoga refers the planetary alignments and their specific results which impact the lives of an individual.

The following list contains yogas in alphabetical order to ease your search.

A

ADHI YOGA

A powerful planetary conjunction created by benefices in the 6th 7th, 7th and 8th houses emanating from the Moon sign. Mercury is not combust , and Jupiter does not create Sakata yoga. This makes a person well-mannered, reliable, and affluent and is able of defeating the enemies of his opponents.

AKHAND SAMRAJYA YOGA

Planetary combinations that provide longevity and prosperity that is triggered with Leo, Scorpio, Aquarius or Taurus as Ascendant. This makes Jupiter govern either the 5th or 11th house in a birth chart.

AMAR YOGA

A powerful planetary conjunction created in two ways

(1) All cardinal houses that are occupied by any malefic and by the benefices of all kinds. In this case, the native is a proprietor of real estate and land In the second instance, he is wealthy and wealthy;

(2) Sun in Aries or Leo occupies the Ascendant or any other trine or cardinal house when Moon is exalted as well as in its sign i.e. it is in Cancer or Taurus as well Jupiter and Venus are in the 8th or 12th houses in the chart of birth. This practice eliminates any negative influences in the horoscope.

## AMARAK YOGA

The planetary conjunction is formed by the 7th house lord situated in the 9th and the 9th lord located in the 7th. both of these planets are strong. It confers on natives large eyes, long arms understanding of religious and legal texts. His wife is loyal to him and he has an upright and moral lifestyle.

## ANAPHA YOGA

Other planets that the Sun which is in the 12th house of the Moon is Anapha yoga. Mars in this location makes the person strong, well-regulated and a leader among those who engage in illegal activities. Mercury helps him to be proficient in oratory and in absorbing conversations. He's also adept in the social arts. Jupiter is a committed and righteous person who spends money for charitable causes. Venus is female, but is revered by those in the position of authority. Saturn can cause disenchantment and the nodes to perversion. The Moon as a yoga guru bestows the well-formed organs as well as good behavior, and self-respect.

ARA SAURI YOGA

The planetary conjunction of Saturn with Mars. It can cause serious ailments.

ARDHA-CHANDRA Yoga

Planetary combination where the planets all occupy houses consecutively with the houses of the cardinals empty. The person in this particular combination is beautiful, happy and has many ornaments, gems, and jewelry.

ARISTHA YOGAS

The planets are a source of misfortune and planetary combinations. These combinations negate positive results and can cause problems. These combinations include:

(i) Malefic connected to the 6th house, 8th and 12th or their lords

(ii) Malefic is a recurring theme on weak Moon

(iii) Sun, Mars (iii) Sun, Mars, and Saturn in the 5th House.

(iv) Mars, Saturn (iv) Saturn, Mars, or Sun in the 8th House.

(v) Malefic aspect of weak ascendant Lord, Sun or Moon

(vi) Sun, Mars, Rahu and Saturn in Ascendant

(vii) Exchange of signals (vii) exchange of signs Jupiter and Mars

(viii) Mars and Saturn in the 2nd House, while Rahu is in the 3rd house.

(ix) Rahu in the 4th as well as Moon in the 6th or 8th houses.

(x) Mars in the 7th house, Venus on the 8th, and Sun in the 9th

(xi) Malice in the 7th and 12th houses.

(xii) Jupiter, Sun, Rahu and Mars occupy significations of malefic planets, and Venus is located in the 7th house.

(xiii) the lord of Ascendant, accompanied by an amalefic or flanked by two malefics and a malefic in the 7th house.

(xiv) Saturn in the 8th house. Moon in Ascendant (xiv) Saturn in the 8th House, Moon in Ascendant, Venus as well. Moon in the 6th or 8th house. (xv) Moon and Mercury in the 8th or 6th house.

## ASHTA LAKSHMI YOGA

In the time that Rahu is in the 6th position and Jupiter is in Kendra this pattern is created. Happiness and wealth are evident.

## AVATARA Yoga

The planetary combination is formed by

(i) the Ascendant is located in the cardinal Sign of Venus or Jupiter in the 1st or 4th, 7th, 8th or 10th houses, as well as

(ii) Saturn in exaltation. This combination can bring spiritual blessings that enrich the heart and mind, allowing him to gain mystic insight and the inner wisdom. He develops into an intelligent and profound student of religion and esoteric writings with psychic sensitivity. This combination can also grant high social standing well-known for meritorious acts and trips to holy and historical sites.

## B

### BAJRA YOGA

The planetary combination that brings all blessings are situated between the first and seventh house in a chart of birth. This makes the person cheerful and fortunate throughout the course time of life.

### BHADRA YOGA

A combination of five that are part of Pancha Mahapurushayoga. Mercury in exaltation , or in its own sign, which is occupying the cardinal house, either from the Ascendant or the Moon creates Bhadrayoga. The combination creates an exemplary behaviour.

A different kind of Bhadrayoga is created through The Moon and Jupiter put within the second house. This is the Lord of the 2nd House in the 11th house and the Ascendant lord , who is associated with benefices. This combination makes the person skilled, intelligent, and adept at understanding the emotions of other people. He is adept in many art forms.

## BHASKARA YOGA

A planetary conjunction that is formed by Mercury situated on the 2nd of the Sun, Moon 11th from Mercury and Jupiter in a trine house with the Moon. Someone born with this combination is strong and powerful, as well as educated. is knowledgeable about the sacred scriptures, mathematics, as well as the classical genre.

## BHAVYA Yoga

The planetary conjunction is created through Moon at the 10th House, the Navamsa Lord from Moon in exaltation and the lord of the 9th house that is linked to the 2nd house lord. This combination makes one wealthy, well-known and educated. He could be famous as a botanist or a collection of ancient artifacts.

## BHERI YOGA

The planetary combination is created in three ways:

(i) all planets are located on the Ascendant, which is located in the second, seventh and 10th house

(ii) Venus and the Lord of Ascendant are located in a cardinal house of the Ascendant and the 9th house lord is strong.

(iii) Venus and the Lord of Ascendant and Jupiter are mutual angles. The 9th house lord is powerful. These combinations result in an person educated in scientific fields as well as practical in daily things, and well-provided with wealth and the comforts of daily life.

## BHUPA YOGA

The planetary conjunction is that is created by the Lord of the 9th or 5th house in the sign where the Navamsa Lord of Rahu is projected to be in its own sign, and is expected to be ruled by Mars. The combination makes the person born under it triumphant in battle and grants him a military standing.

## C

## CHAKRA Yoga

Planetary conjunction that is formed through Rahu during the 10th Lord of the 10th house as well as Ascendant Lord in the 9th house. This makes the person the head of a particular region. He leads his army. He is widely appreciated. In addition, all planets in odd houses starting with Ascendant can also create Chakra Yoga. It confers a high social standing to the person.

## CHAMAR YOGA

A planetary combination where the Ascendant Lord in exaltation is located in a cardinal home that is ruled by Jupiter. In the event that two benefices reside in the Ascendant 7th, 9th or the 10th homes, Chamar Yoga is formed. This makes the person wise and philosophical as well as a great orator. This kind of person is usually born into a royal lineage.

## CHANDRA Yoga

The planetary combination is constituted by an exalted star in ascendant that is expected by Mars and the 9th house's lord is on the house of 3rd. This makes the person a leader the role of an adviser or commanding officer in an army. The person is brave and can last for more than six decades.

## CHANDRA MANGALA YOGA

If Mars is in the 7th position or is in conjunction with Moon this yoga develops. This signifies more land-based properties, reputation and prosperity for the person who is born. Stress and anxiety are as well.

## CHANDRIKA Yoga

A planetary conjunction in which the Ascendant is the Lord of the sign within that the 9th Lord also located, while Mars is situated on the 5th house. People born under this sign have power, and can achieve the highest social status in their lives, but don't have issues with men.

## CHAPA YOGA

It is an planetary conjunction in which all planets reside in the 10th to 4th houses. People born under this sign are skilled thieves, and are generally disliked. Chapa Yoga is also formed in the event that you are born when the Sun occurs located in Aquarius, Mars in Aries and Jupiter is in its particular sign. This can make the person a world traveler.

## CHATURMUKH YOGA

The planetary combination is formed in the form of Jupiter inside a cardinal home in the sign of the 9th house lord, Venus in a cardinal house that is related to the sign of the Lord of the 11th House as well as the Ascendant lord and the lord of 10th house, themselves placed within the houses of cardinals. This makes the person proficient and successful in his endeavors and well-respected. He has plenty of materials and enjoys an extremely long time.

## CHATURSAGAR Yoga

The planetary combination is created by all planets positives and negatives and cardinal houses. It brings wealth, prosperity as well as a high-status throughout life. A person who is famous after his death.

## CHHATRA YOGA

The planetary combination is made up of all planets that are located in the seven first house on the chart. This makes the person satisfied from the beginning of his life until the end.

## D

## DANDA YOGA

The planetary conjunction can be formed in a variety of ways. If Venus aligns with Jupiter situated in the 3rd House, while the lord of 3rd is elevated, Danda Yoga is formed. It can also occur in the event that all planets have been solely within Gemini, Cancer, Virgo, Sagittarius and Pisces signs. Danda Yoga makes a person well-known, extremely wealthy and a competent administrator and a religious person.

A negative combination in the name occurs when all planets reside in the 11th, 10th, as well as the 12th house. Iit renders the individual poor and dependent on others for his livelihood and rejected by his family and friends.

DARIDRA YOGA

The planetary system produces indigence as well as personal ailments. These are:

(i) Jupiter as lord of the 8th house or 1st house is stronger than the strength of the lord of 9th house. Likewise, the Lord of the 11th house is not the cardinal house or is in a combust

(ii) Combust and debilitated Jupiter, Mars, Saturn or Mercury is located on the 6th, 11th 8th, 12th or 5th Bhava

(iii) Saturn in 9th house is influenced by malefic planets. Mercury is connected to the Sun and is located in the Ascendant. In addition, it is associated with the Sun. Pisces the Navamsa

(iv) Jupiter, Mercury, Venus, Saturn, and Mars are located in any order 8th 6th, 12th, 5th and

10th Bhavas and the 12th house lord which is weakened by the sun's aspect, has more power than the Ascendant lord.

(v) (v) Venus, Jupiter, Moon and Mars can be found in any four of the 1st, 10st 11th and 6th and 8th Bhavas

(vi) Venus in Ascendant in debilitation and Jupiter, Mars, and Moon are also suffering from debilitation.

(vii) (vii) The Ascendant lies in the cardinal sign and it is rising. Navamsa is in the midst of Saturn and is depressed Jupiter

(viii) (viii) Jupiter is in the 6th or 8th Bhava in a sign that is not being its own

(ix) Ascendant in a fixed sign malefic in trine and cardinal houses, strong angles that are devoid of benefits

(x) The night time of birth. ascendant to a cardinal sign weak benefics reside in angles and trine. They are malefics not in the cardinal houses.

The people that are born into Daridra Yoga suffer deprivations of different intensity and face difficult and difficult conditions in life. They earn their money through illegal methods. Their life in social circles is not honorable. They experience unexpectedly in their lives.

DATA YOGA

Planetary combinations made up of Jupiter ascendant Venus within the 4th, Mercury within the seventh as well as Mars located in the 9th. This combination makes one wealthy and generous.

## DEVENDRA YOGA

The planetary combination is formed by the Ascendant under a fixed constellation the Ascendant Lord in 11.11th, Lord in 11th as Ascendant, and the lords of the 2nd and 10th houses of mutual exchange. This combination is effective to make the person attractive, loved by beautiful women, possessor of enormous fortune and luxurious villas. He is able to achieve a impressive social standing.

## DHARMA YOGA

The planetary conjunction is created by the conjunction of Jupiter and Venus together with the 2nd lord on the 9th. This makes the person extremely religious, devoted to war as well as a chivalrous leader of an entire army. The person also grows rich and generous.

## DURUDHARA Yoga

Planetary combination based on planets that are located on opposite sides of the Moon. They usually bring wealth like wealth, comforts in life, and a high social standing. Sun and nodes need not be part of this particular combination. If Moon is in a symbiosis with Mars and

Mercury the combination renders the person cruel, greedy and fond of old women and a deceiver. Mars and Jupiter when in this position makes the person famous, smart and wealthy and also an ally to others against opponents. Venus and Mars can make a person a lover of battle, intense physical effort, and bold actions. When you combine Saturn and Mars one becomes an expert in the field of sexual art and is able to accumulate a wealth of money. is a slave to a hectic lifestyle and is constantly confronted by adversaries. Combining Jupiter and Mercury confers a sense of religious zeal, knowledge of scriptures, general wealth and fame. Mercury and Venus in this situation makes an individual attractive, beautiful confident, wealthy, and a recipient of professional standing. Moon situated the area between Saturn and Mercury permits the individual to travel around the world to seek riches. Jupiter and Venus create a person who is more patient, intelligent balanced, ethical, and balanced He is able to acquire jewelry, fame, and a an administrative job that is well-known. If Venus and Saturn are paired and allow the individual to obtain an elderly spouse from a well-known family, making the person skilled in many trades appreciated by women and well-liked by officials from the government. Saturn and Jupiter accompanying the Moon cause a lot of problems in the private life of the person who is frequently beset by scandals, controversies and legal disputes, yet they are not harmed.

Durudhara Yoga makes the individual comfortable in their physical body and wealth, as well as loyal assistants and genuine followers, however towards the end of the individual's life, there's an overwhelming desire to give up the material objects.

## DWAJA YOGA

A planetary combo made up of all the negative energies that are placed in the 8th House and all benefices that are in the ascendant. With this configuration, an individual leader will be born under this combination.

## E

## EKAWALI YOGA

A planetary combination where the planets are in various houses in a sequential way. This makes the person an Emperor.

## G

## GADA YOGA

The planetary combination is formed by two methods:

(i) Moon placed in the 2nd House together with Jupiter and Venus or the 9th house lord facing them and

(ii) all planets including the nodes, are located in the cardinal houses that are adjacent. Gada Yoga makes the individual involved in religious and philanthropic actions, but imposing in appearance and unaffected by any enemies. He earns a good amount of income. He also has a happy marriage.

## GAJA YOGA

Planetary combination where the Lord of the 7th house is born from Ascendant which is 9th in the 11th house is located in the 11th place along with the Moon and the Lord of the 11th House aligns with these two. People born in this type of combination is always content blessed, wealthy, and religious and is a lavish person.

## GAJA KESARI-YOGA

Planetary combinations are formed by the specific relationships with Moon as well as Jupiter. It suggests that Jupiter is in an angle with respect to Moon as well as the Ascendant. It also suggests that benefics like Venus, Jupiter, and Mercury without being destroyed or debilitated are in opposition to the Moon. Another possibility is that Jupiter within a square from the Ascendant , or Moon is associated with or anticipated by benefics that are not either combust or placed to the house of the 6th. This combination makes the individual wealthy, bright, intelligent well-off and loved by the state. The practice is both safe against the evil effects of others evil forces, as well as producing of positive results.

## GO-YOGA

Planetary conjunction formed by the an elevation of the lord of the Ascendant, as well as powerful Jupiter located within its Mool Trikona, in conjunction with the Lord of the second house. This makes the person hail from a wealthy family and confers on his beauty, happiness and a high social standing.

## GURU CHANDALAYOGA YOGA

A planetary conjunction that relates Jupiter with Rahu. If these two planets are paired in a house, it results in negative outcomes. The person is vulnerable and prone to engage in morally, socially, and sexually unmoral actions.

## H

## HALA YOGA

It is triggered when all planets are situated within a cluster of triangular houses that are not the Ascendant.According to another interpretation it is believed that all planets located in the 9th and 5th houses are also responsible for the formation of Halayoga. The people born under this particular combination are involved in agriculture in a significant way.

## HAMSA YOGA

One of the Maha Purusha Yogas that are created by Jupiter in exaltation or its own constellation and power, occupying a cardinal home whether from the Ascendant sign or The Moon sign. The person who is fortunate as well-built and with the voice that of the Swan. He has a gorgeous wife and is a complete ease. He is a religious person and adroitly disposed to spiritual pursuits. This combination is believed to bring about a lifespan longer than an 82-year span.

HARIHARA BRAHMAYOGA

We're talking about three sets of combinations of planets:

(i) Benefics that are placed on the second, eighth and 12th houses, starting from the sign that the Lord of the 2nd home is located.

(ii) Jupiter, Moon (iii) Jupiter, Moon Mercury are posited in the 9th, 4th and 8th houses, respectively. the sign in which the Lord 7th house located.

(iii) (iii) the Sun, Venus and Mars in the 4th, 10th or 11 house of the Ascendant Lord. The combination makes the person honest, powerful speaker and a victor, knowledgeable about religious texts, and philanthropic.

I

ICHCHITA MRITYU YOGA

The planetary conjunction is made by Mars in the cardinal house, and Rahu within the seventh. The individual is destined to self-destruct.

IKKBALA YOGA

A term that is used in forecasting annual events. It is created by the placement of all planets within Panphara houses. It is the source of many occasions throughout the year.

INDUVARA Yoga

The planetary conjunction. 7 planets (excluding Rahu and Ketu) in a horoscope that is progressed, that is based on the solar ingress principle that are located in Apoklima houses create obstacles , which hinder the potential of an auspicious combination that could otherwise exist.

K

KAHAL YOGA

A planetary combination that can produce contradictions: people born in the combination are brave, virtuous with a well-equipped military and governing vast areas, but they are insular or inexperienced. The combination is formed in a variety of ways. The Lords of the 9th and 4th houses need to coincide, and that of the ascendant must be robust. The combo can also be formed by the fact that the lord from the 4th is in its own exaltation or sign and is believed to be expected by or together with the 10th lord.

KALANIDHI Yoga

Planetary combination created by Jupiter in the 5th or 2nd home, Mercury and Venus expecting or joining with it. A person born under this combination is adored by a variety of heads of state. He grows wealthy, successful and healthy, and is in the top position in the world.

KALASARPA YOGA

If all planets are located in the vicinity of Rahu and Ketu this yoga forms. Even though the planets that are favorable are located between them or in their own house, this is a power. This is a negative yoga. The majority of the time, the first half of your life is filled with struggles.

KAMAL YOGA

The planetary combination is made up of the planets that are located in 1st 4th, 7th, 7th and 10th houses, which will make the person born under it famous as happy and successful in various fields.

KAMBOOLA Yoga

The planetary conjunction is created by Ithasala relationship between the Lord of the ascendant and the 10th house lord particularly where one is connected to Moon.

It is believed that the Kamboola Yoga is of 3 types, Shrestha (the best), Madhyama (ordinary) and Adhama (the most harmful) according to the strength of the planets that are involved.

## KANDUKA YOGA

The planetary combination is formed from the lord in 10th located in the 9th house, Lord of the 2nd house in Ascendant, as well as the 2nd and 10th house posited by benefics. The person born in this type of combination is a good person but extremely materialistic in his way of living life. He is in search of enjoyment from every kind of physical comfort and an extravagant lifestyle.

## KARAGAR YOGA

Planetary combination created by one or two malefic planets that are not influenced by any benefics and located at the same time in 2-12, 3-11 or in 4-10 homes. This can lead to the possibility of detention or imprisonment. Similar outcomes can also be seen when malefics are located in 12th or 9th houses.

## KAHAL YOGA

The planetary combination can result in opposite results: those born under this combination are brave and virtuous with a well-equipped military and governing vast areas, but they are intellectually naive in their thinking, uninformed and lacking common sense and garden guts. The combination can be interpreted by a variety of methods: the most well-known version states that the lords from the 9th and 4th houses must have mutual angle, and those who are the ascendant must be solid. The combination also occurs by the fact that the lord of 4th houses is elevated or has its own sign, and is expected by or in conjunction in conjunction with 10th lord.A person born under this sign is wealthy and benevolent, respectful and God-fearing. He is joyful, generous, and elegant in appearance.

KEDAR YOGA

The planetary combination is created by all planets that are located in four houses on a birth chart. The individual is willing to fight an enlightened war, embark on an appropriate mission, adhere to the traditional religion and practices, and be patient, humble and philanthropic. He is also keen on agriculture and valued within his community.

KEMA DRUMA YOGA

Planetary combinations are created by Moon in the absence of being bound by any planet on its sides. Sun isn't part of this particular combination. It is also necessary to allow Moon to be part of this mix and that no planet be located in a cardinal position in the horoscope. This makes the person without any education or ability. He is a victim of poverty and faces many challenges in his life.

## KESARI YOGA

If Jupiter as well as Moon are in Kendra, mutually, this yoga can be formed. Particularly during the times when Jupiter occurs in Kendra 7th through Moon (bright phase Moon) the yoga takes shape. Fame, wealth, and name are created.

## KSHEMA YOGA

Planetary conjunction made by the lord of the Ascendant, as well as the lords of the 8th 9th, 10th and 9th houses that are occupying their own sign. The individual is able to be able to support his family members and other family members. He is financially prosperous and happy, and lives the rest of his life.

## KURMA YOGA

Planetary combinations created by benefics of the 5th and 6th houses, either in exaltation or their own signs, of planets that are friendly, or in the navamsas of planets that are friendly. It can also be formed when the benefics are located situated in the Ascendant, 3rd and 11th houses that are in exaltation, their own signs or their Mool Trikona places. People born in this yoga are leaders, highly acclaimed and helpful, as well as charitable and lead a joyful life.

## KUSUMA YOGA

Planetary conjunction made up of Saturn in the 10th house. Venus is placed in a cardinal house that has fixed signs, and an fragile Moon inside a trine. Alternately, Jupiter should be in ascendant, Moon in the 7th and Sun occupies the 8th spot from Moon (that is located on the 2nd house in this case). People that are blessed with the combination come from an aristocratic family. They achieve high standing in society and have a charitable attitude and a pristine appearance.

KUTA YOGA

The planetary combination is formed by the placement of all planets in succession between the 4th and 10th house. The individual is able to live in mountainous or forest areas and they can be very cruel and obnoxious.

L

LAKSHMI YOGA

Planetary conjunction created by a powerful Ascendant Lord, also known as the lord of the 9th, in its own exaltation, or is a trine sign which is located in a cardinal house. The people born under it are beautiful spiritual and wealthy. They are also accomplished, well-off famed, and have high standing in society. The offspring of these are extremely bright.

M

MADAN YOGA

The planetary combination is a result of the Lord of the 10th House as a constellation in the Ascendant, along together with Venus along with the lord from the the 11th which is located in the 11th house. It makes an person born under it attractive and well-known in the world of politics. He starts to flourish at an young age of just twenty years old.

## MAHA PATAKA YOGA

A planetary alignment that is formed by Moon closely associated with Rahu and is influenced by Jupiter conjunct to malefic. It causes the person who is highly educated and well-established in the society, to indulge in savage behavior and actions.

## MAHAPURUSHA YOGAS

Planetary patterns that symbolize the maturity in the spiritual. They occur when any of the five stars which are Saturn, Jupiter, Mars, Mercury and Venus, with strength, is in their own exaltation or friendly sign that is identical to the cardinal houses. The planets create five types of notable people. the combination is known by the names of Sasa, Ruchaka, Bhadra, Hamsa, and Malavya yogas resulting from Saturn, Mars, Mercury, Jupiter, and Venus and Jupiter, respectively. These types of combinations allow the person to free himself from uncontrollable actions, and to focus one's focused efforts toward specific goals in one's life.

MALA YOGA

Planetary combinations created by the lords of the 2nd 7th, 9th, 7th and 11th houses, positioned under their respective sign. It confers high-level administrative status to the person and makes the person a minister or a treasurer of the royal family or leader of the masses. The fortune of the individual increases when he reaches reaching the age of 32.

MALAVYA Yoga

One of the five planets combinations that promote human supremeness, Panch Maha Purusha Yoga was created by Venus as a symbol of exaltation in the occupation of her own sign and located in a cardinal home. This makes the person the head of an cultural institution, giving the person a lifespan that is 70 years. The person dies in an abode of worship, where they practice penance and yoga.

The person with Malavya Yoga possesses a graceful appearance with the luster Moon. He is slim with a wide waist, beautiful lips long hands, a deep voice, and well-shaped teeth. He is happy to live to the age of.

MARUD Yoga

Planetary combinations are made through Jupiter in a trine-house made up of Venus,

Moon in 5th from Jupiter and Sun in a cardinal home in relation to Moon. The combination makes the individual very wealthy and also a successful businessman.

## MATSYA YOGA

The planetary combination is formed by benefics and malefics in the 5th house. malefic in the Ascendant as well as in the 9th house, and malefic that is in the 4th or 8th house, which is the Ascendant's. People born in this particular combination is religious, compassionate smart and well-known.

## MRIGA Yoga

The planetary combination is created through the placement of Navamsa Lord of the 8th House in an auspicious position, along with an auspicious planet and the Lord of the 9th house in glory. This makes the person well-known, rich, charitable and powerful in character.

## MUKUTA YOGA

A planetary conjunction that is formed in the 9th house by Jupiter within the 9th House, which is the sign of the 9th house lord and a benefic that is positioned in the 9th house by Jupiter as well as Saturn within the house of 10th, which is located from the ascendant. People born under this type of combination has farms and forests, and becomes the leader of tribespeople and is well-read. He is well-educated, but harsh in temperament. His success begins at an early age.

MUSALA YOGA

A planetary conjunction created by all planets in fixed signs or , alternatively, Rahu in the 10th house, which is the Lord of the 10th house , in the throne of glory and feared by Saturn. It makes those born under it extremely wealthy with permanent assets. He is a consultant to the government, or an enterprise that is a major commercial one or has a high standing in the administration.

N

NABHI YOGA

Planetary conjunction made through Jupiter within the 9th House. It is lord of the 9th House in the 11th house from Jupiter, i.e., 7th from Ascendant and Moon connected to Jupiter. This combination gives those born under it a favorable outlook throughout their lives, particularly when they reach the age of 25 years. Additionally, he is awarded numerous honors from the government and accumulates a huge amount of fortune.

NAGA YOGA

Planetary conjunction that is created by the Lord of the Navamsa sign of the 10th house, occupying the 10th house together with the ascendant Lord. Anyone born under this combination receives education, especially at reaching the age of sixteen. In the end, he receives honors from the state as well as wealth. Because of his temperament, he is courteous.

## NAGENDRA YOGA

Planetary conjunction formed by the position of the 9th house lord in the 3rd House that is being that is inspected by Jupiter. This makes the person physically well-balanced, pleasant and well-educated. The prosperity of the individual increases at the age of 6 years old.

## NAKTYA YOGA

The planetary combination is used in the Tajaka system. It is related to the relationship between planets that have different motions in close proximity. When the Lord of the ascendant and the house lord which is the subject of study don't have a mutual aspect however, there is a fast-moving planet between them the fast-moving planet between them will transfer the positive influence of the earlier planet to the forward.

## NALA YOGA

Planetary combination triggered the exaltation of the Lord of Navamsa sign, in which the the ninth house situated and is associated with the Ascendant Lord. This makes the person strong after seven year old age. He is awarded numerous state awards and is fascinated by the Bible.

NALIKA YOGA

The planetary combination is created by the positioning of the Lord of the 5th House in the 9th house. The 11th house lord occupies the 2nd floor along with the Moon. The combination makes one extremely creative and a great speaker.

NANDA YOGA

A planetary conjunction made up of two planets from both signs, as well as one planet from every sign. It confers prosperity and a longer life.

NASIR YOGA

Planetary combinations are created by the Ascendant Lord and Jupiter located in the 4th house. Moon connected to the 7th house's lord and the Ascendant is influenced by an benefic. The person born in this type of combination is extremely charitable and well-proportioned but bulky in body. He is renowned when he reaches his age, which is 33.

NAU YOGA

A planetary union created by all planets that occupy successively seven of the houses with any gaps. The person earns his living from jobs associated to fishing, navigation export, import and international trade.

## NEECHABHANGA RAJA YOGA

The planetary combination allows the cancellation of the negative effects of the planet that is debilitated. The cancellation allows the person to be elevated to the status of King. The mixture can be formed in a variety of ways like

(i) the planet born in its depressive state is the lord of the sign, or its exaltation sign cardinal house in relation to the Moon or ascendant sign

(ii) the Lord of the Navamsa is occupied by the depressed planet when born placed in a cardinal house or in the trine house in relation to the Ascendant. The Ascendant Lord itself is the Navamsa belonging to a movable sign.

## NRIPA Yoga

The planetary conjunction is created by the lord of Navamsa sign of Ascendant that is associated with the Lord of Moon sign as well as the Lord of the 10th house that is a part of it. Anyone born under this particular combination has an extremely high position in the world and is widely famous. The Yoga is a fruitful practice that begins very early in life.

## O

## OBHAYACHARI Yoga

Planetary combination created by the planets apart from Moon that are located on the opposite sides of Sun. This makes one balanced, attractive, and efficient in various tasks and full of energy and tolerant. They are also well-balanced in dealing with complex issues. A person who is wealthy like a king, is in healthy and is able to enjoy all positive aspects of life.

P

PADMA YOGA

Planetary conjunction made by the lords from the 9th house coming from Ascendant and Moon placed together in the 7th house of Venus. The people born into this combination are extremely content have a luxurious lifestyle and engage in a variety of positive activities. When they reach the age of fifteen years, they receive special treatment by the state as well as the elderly.

PAKSHIN YOGA

A planetary conjunction that is created by all planets within the 10th house and 4th. The individual is an ambassador for messages. it could even make him an ambassador. He'd be unpopular and always on the move.

PANCHA MAHAPURUSHA YOGA

Planetary combinations created by non-luminaries Mars, Mercury, Jupiter, Venus, and Saturn in their own signs or exaltation, and occupying an astrological cardinal house. Each of these non-luminaries form the yoga on their own and has its own name and an effect. Ruchaka yoga is created by the combination that includes Mars, Bhadra by Mercury, Hamsa by Jupiter, Malavya by Venus along with Sasa Yoga in the direction of Saturn.

## PARIVARTHANA YOGA

This refers to that mutual houses can be exchanged. Two lords can swap their homes. If the 9th lord exchanges will exchange, this could result in excellent results. If the lords are 5 and 10 exchanges or seven and 10-exchange, or 5,9 exchange, very positive results are evident. Even if the lord of 10 is in 9th or 9th in the 10th, this yoga can be created in part. In the event that the lord of the 10th has an part of the lord in 5 or 9 is present, this yoga may be formed to an extent.

Ruchaka Yoga: Strong physique and well-versed in the traditional love, abides by the customs and traditions and is a household name. This kind of person is also rich and long-lived and manages the men in a group and/or an armies.

Bhadra Yoga: Strong body with a lion's-like face. The person is friendly to family members and achieves an intellectually superior status.

Hamsa Yoga: A righteous person who is graceful in appearance, thoughtful dedicated to gods and higher values and a ritualist in religious practices.

Malavya Yoga: Essentially a family-oriented person who is occupied with household chores and with grandchildren and children. He owns a personal car and a residence as well as other things that are essential to life.

Sasa Yoga: Sensuous, spiritualist, leader of occultists or antisocial groups. Unflinching and capable of performing brutal acts.

PAPAKARTRI YOGA

The malefic planets that surround any planet or house. It ruins the auspiciousness of the respective planets and confers malefic influences. The home or planet that is affected does not flourish.

PARIJATA YOGA

A planetary conjunction that is linked to the Ascendant's position Lord. If the god of the sign where the Ascendant Lord is located or if the Lord of the navamsa in which the is the lord of the sign which the Ascendant lord's set is located in the cardinal or trine houses,

Parijata Yoga is formed. It is a means of making the person born as a sovereign who is likely to be content in the latter or middle period of their lives. A person who is a sovereign is admired by the other sovereigns. He is a lover of fighting, has a wealth of a million dollars but is cognizant of his obligations towards the stateand gentle in his disposition.

PARIVRAJYA YOGA

Asceticism on the planet is a combination of planets. Ascetic yogas that are important are:

(i) (ii) Four or more planets of strength that are in one house, with Raja Yoga present in the Horoscope

(ii) The Lord of the Moon sign, which has no aspect of its own, faces Saturn or Saturn is in opposition to the Lord of the sign that is that is occupied by the Moon that is also fragile

(iii) Moon occupies drekkana of Saturn and is expected by Saturn. A person who does this is averse to the world and routine relationships

(iv) Moon occupies the navamsa of Saturn or Mars and is regarded as a sign of Saturn or Mars. by Saturn. The person in question is bored of the everyday life and leads an esoteric life.

(v) Jupiter, Moon and the Ascendant anticipated by Saturn and Jupiter being in the 9th house of the horoscope, make someone who was born within Raja Yoga a holy and legendary creator of a system of philosophical thought.

(vi) Saturn unaccepted by the 9th House, and there are Raja Yoga in the horoscope. The combination can make the person join a holy order and be the lord of men.

PARVAT YOGA

These planetary combinations are of two varieties. First, benefics within the cardinal house of Ascendant as well as the 6th and 8th houses that are either placed by benefics or empty. The Ascendant lord and the lord of the 12th house each in cardinal houses apart separated from one another, and are favored by planets with friendly relations. People born under these constellations are blessed, and are adept at learning about different topics, and are generous and caring. They are social or political leaders. However, they also are a magnet for women.

PASHA YOGA

The people born under it make a lot of money and are highly competent and well-known.

PRESHYA Yoga

Combinations of planets that lead to servitude are formed

(i) If the Sun occurs in the 10th House, Moon is in the 7th house, Saturn at the end of the 4th Mars on the third and Ascendant is the cardinal sign, while Jupiter is located on the second house. The people born under this combo in the night will be servants of another.

(ii) (iii) Venus is in the 9th place, Moon the 7th house, Mars the 8th, and Jupiter occupies the 2nd House or the Ascendant, the Ascendant lies in a fixed sign. A person born in this particular combination is always in the service of others.

(iii) (iii) was born in the night and is a Lord of the rising movable sign of Sandhi and a planet that is located in a cardinal house.

(iv) Jupiter attains Iravathamsa and is in an Sandhi (iv) Jupiter is Iravathamsa and resides in a Sand Moon is not in a cardinal house , but has Uttam-varga. Venus has the sign of rising. Her birth occurs in the evening during the dark portion of the lunar month. The person born is menial

(v) If at the time of the birth of a person Mars, Jupiter, and Sun each occupy the Sandhis of the 6th 4, and 10th Bhavas (v) or

(vi) (vi) Moon when it is in an Amsa (q.v.) or a planet that is malefic, is in the Benefic sign or

(vii) If Jupiter occurs to be in Capricorn in the 6th, 8th or 12th bhava, and the Moon has entered the fourth bhava, which is Rising sign - the person born will need to perform at the bidding of other people.

R

RAJA/RAJYAYOGA

The planetary combination that creates wealth, affluence and royalty. The most important Rajya Yogas are as follows:

(i) The mutual relationship (ii) Mutual relationship Karakamsa with Ascendant.

(ii) Ascendant 2nd, 4th and houses that are associated with benefics, and the 3rd home is occupied by malefic.

(iii) (iii) The 2nd house is could be occupied by one or all of the planets Moon, Jupiter, Venus or a powerful Mercury that are in their own signs.

(iv) The planets that are debilitated in the 6th,8th and 3rd houses. the Ascendant lord is in its own or the exaltation sign within the Ascendant.

(v) Lord of 10th House while in its own house or with its exaltation sign faces the ascendant.

(vi) All benefices are located in cardinal houses.

(vii) Lords with debilitation from the 8th, 6th and 12th houses face the ascendant.

(viii) Any relation between the Lords of the 5th and 9th houses.

(ix) The alliance of the lords of 5th, 10th and 4th houses as well as Ascendant to the lord from the 9th house.

(x) Lord of 5th House with the Lord of the 9th house or the Ascendant Lord of the 4th, 1st or the 10th house.

(xi) Venus associated with Jupiter in the 9th house, if it falls under an aspect of Sagittarius or Pisces or the Lord in the fifth house.

(xii) Moon in the 3rd or 11th houses, and Venus in the 11th or 3rd house, and Venus. in the 7th House from it.

Numerous other beneficial combinations like Gaja Kesari Yoga, Pancha Maha Purusha Yoga and Lakshmi Yoga are also important Rajya Yogas.

## RAJAPADA YOGA

Combination made through Moon as well as Ascendant of Vargottama Navamsa and the four or more planets that are expecting these. It creates the head of the state or its equivalent.

RAJJU YOGA

The planetary combination is created by all the planets that are movable signs. The combination forces the person born under it move to a different country. He is usually unfair and engages in illicit actions.

RASATALA Yoga

The planetary conjunction is formulated by the 12th house lord in exaltation, as well as Venus is positioned within the 12th house, and aligned with the 4th house lord. The people born under it gain the status of being the head of the state. There is a chance that they will find riches beneath the earth.

RAVI YOGA

The combination of planets is formed through Sun within the 10th House as well as the Lord of the 10th house in the 3rd house, together with Saturn. The person who is born in this particular combination an Scientist who is able to achieve a high position in the field of management. He is not hungry and is very absorbed in his research, and is highly valued.

REKHA YOGA

A planetary conjunction that causes poverty. It happens when the weak Lord of Ascendant is influenced by the 8th house lord and Jupiter is combusted by Sun. In addition, you are a lord in Navamsa that is the 4th house lord can be obscured due to Sun while Sun itself is aspected by the 12th house lord.

## S

### SAKATA YOGA

Planetary combinations are described in various ways in texts of classical origin. It is created by all the planets within the 1st and 7th house which makes the person choose the lowest occupations. It can also occur when Jupiter is in the position of 6th or 8th from the Moon located in a place that is not the cardinal house with respect to the ascendant. This can lead to poverty for those born into the royal family. A person who is in this situation will be plagued for the rest of his life and is resentful of the heads of state. Moon located in the 12th or 8th or the 6th house of Jupiter is the cause of Sakata Yoga, unless Moon is in a cardinal home. The person who is born with this combination will lose his wealth or place in life, but gains these. Sakata Yoga produces cyclic fluctuation in fortune, similar to the wheels of a horse turning around its center of gravity.

### SAMRAJYA YOGA

Planetary conjunction created by the lord of the Navamsa sign of the 9th house's lord and

Jupiter who is in the 2nd House. This makes the person an administrative officer of the highest rank living in the luxuries of.

## SAMUDRA YOGA

A planetary combination that is formed by all planets within houses that are even, such as the 2nd 4th, 6th and so on. The odd houses, like the 3rd, 1st and so on. are not occupied. This combination brings fame to the person, and they are offered all the conveniences of daily life.

## SANKHYA Yoga

Based on the amount of the signs occupied by the seven planets, Sankhya Yoga is formed. The diverse combinations that result from the houses occupied are given various names.

(a) Vina Yoga (seven signs occupied);

(b) Dama Yoga (six signs occupied);

(c) Pasha Yoga (five signs occupied);

(d) Kedar Yoga (four signs occupied);

(e) Shula Yoga (three signs occupied);

(f) Yuga Yoga (two signs occupied); and

(g) Gola Yoga (one sign occupied).

The results are produced regardless of the other yoga that is created by these combinations, such as Chap Yoga, Kshetri Yoga, Nav Yoga, etc. are not observed.

## SASA Yoga

One of the Yogas of Panch Maha Purusha. It is created by an extremely powerful Saturn who is in a cardinal house in conjunction with the sign of exaltation. The individual is able to command several Retirees. His libidinous inclination is uncontrollable. He is a king over a territory. He is mentally at a moment where a drastic change in his behavior is in the near future disillusionment with the sex world may lead him to spirituality. It is possible that he will be a more desire-driven donor.

SHAKTI YOGA

A planetary combination that is created by all planets in the seventh, eighth 9th and 10th houses. This makes a person poor and devoid of money and pleasure, yet the person gains great proficiency in arguing on behalf of criminal litigants.

SHANKHA YOGA

Planetary combinations are formed in two ways,(i) the Lords from the 6th and 5th houses that are located in the cardinal houses are separated from one another and the Ascendant strong as is (ii) the ascendant lords as well as the house of 10th are placed in movable signs , while the 9th house's lord is powerful. The combination of these houses makes the person born under them, well-educated in the Bible and principles, a person of character and morality, and involved in noble actions. They live the longest lives.

## SHAR YOGA

The planetary combination is formed by the alignment of all planets within the fourth, fifth sixth and seventh house. It can make the person born in it cruel conditions and is associated to prisons.

## SHARDA YOGA

Planetary combination is formed by two different ways

(i) the Lord of the 10th house, positioned in the 5th place, Mercury located in a cardinal home, and Sun or within its sign, or in a powerful place and

(ii) Jupiter situated in the trine house of Moon as well as Mars in a trine home from Mercury. In these combination the person is well behaved, dependable and God-fearing. They are respected by the state.

## V

## VASUMATI YOGA

Planetary combinations made by Venus, Jupiter and Mercury as long as Mercury doesn't have any evil or negative Upachaya house that is ascendant or with the Moon.

This creates the possibility for an person to become a billionaire.

## VASI YOGA
Planet 12th to Sun this yoga develops Naming and fame the indications.

## VESI YOGA
Other planets than Moon which occupies the 2nd House of the Sun sign creates Vesi Yoga; a similar placement in the 12th House results in Vasi Yoga. If Sun sign is surrounded by planets that are not Moon in both pairs, it creates Ubhayachari Yoga. The people who are born in Vesi Yoga are truthful, poor, lazy and uninvolved. Vasi Yoga produces individuals skilled in a variety of arts. They are generous, strong educated, well-known, and dazzling.

## VIBHAVASU YOGA
A planetary conjunction made up of Mars either exalted or put in the 10th House, with exalted Sun within the second house and Moon in conjunction in conjunction with Jupiter located in the 9th. The person born under this combination to marry a lovely woman and enjoy a pleasant life. He will be prosperous and have an elevated position in the life of.

## VIDYUTA YOGA

Planetary conjunction that is created by the Lord of the 11th house exaltation with Venus in a cardinal house in relation to the house that is occupied by the Ascendant Lord. It makes the individual generous and wealthy and allows him to enjoy an enviable position in the world.

VISHNU YOGA

The combination formed by the Lords of the 9th and 10th houses and the lord of Navamsa sign 9th lord who is positioned on the 2nd House. This makes the person highly favored from the government. In nature, he's intelligent, patient proficient in debate and is a lively and engaging speaker. He is rich and stays for a long time.

Y

YAV YOGA

The planetary combination is created by all malefics in the 1st and 7th houses, and all benefics within the 10th and 4th houses. This makes the person strong and his middle-time of life is blissfully happy.

YUGMA YogA

A planetary conjunction that was created by the Lord of the 4th, 9th with a positive and Jupiter anticipating it. The person born under this particular combination gets important gifts from the government and those in power and enjoys a pleasant and prosperous life.

YUP Yoga

The planetary combination is made by all planets of the Ascendant, 2nd, 3rd and 4th houses. The individual is spiritual, charitable, and generous and performs many important rituals.

www.ingramcontent.com/pod-product-compliance
Lightning Source LLC
Chambersburg PA
CBHW050026130526
44590CB00042B/1918